Our Hearts at Sunday Mass

Our Hearts at Sunday Mass

Ten Steps to a Joyful Life

Alan Phillip, C.P.

Passionist Community Press
Sierra Madre, California

Spirit of Hope Publishing
Irvine, California

OUR HEARTS AT SUNDAY MASS: Ten Steps to a Joyful Life
Copyright © 2009 Alan Phillip, C.P.
Published by Spirit of Hope Publishing

International Standard Book Number 978-1-929753-06-2
Printed in the United States of America

Written by Alan Phillip
Developmental Editing by Jerry Seiden
Copy Editing by Chelese Palmer
Front Cover Photo by Steve Pulone
Back Cover Photo by Anthony Montesione
Illustrations by Joseph Roy

NOTE: This book is designed to provide information on the subject matter
covered. It is provided with the understanding that the publisher and author are not
engaged in rendering individualized professional services. If medical advice or
other expert assistance is required, the services of a competent professional should
be sought. The checklists in this book are not designed to substitute for
professional evaluations or psychotherapy.

The anecdotal illustrations and personal stories in this book are composites of real
situations or personal recollections in which facts may have been altered, liberties
taken, and/or names changed to protect the privacy of certain individuals.

For information & permission contact:
Spirit of Hope Publishing
PO Box 53642, Irvine, CA 92619-3642
Phone: 714-308-2494
Website: www.SpiritofHopePublishing.com

DEDICATION

*To my parents who first
showed me the ways of faith*

ACKNOWLEDGMENTS

$\mathcal{I}$t is impossible to acknowledge all the people who inspired this book. But I am especially grateful for the following:

Sr. Bonfilia, CSFN, who taught me how to serve Mass; Msgr. William Stoeckel, Fr. William Quinlan and Fr. Donald Ahearn, whom I served as an altar boy.

Fr. Jerome Stowell, C.P., and Fr. Aidan Kavanaugh, O.S.B., who taught me about liturgy in my seminary years; and Fr. Claude Nevin, C.P., who taught me how to appreciate and sing Gregorian Chant.

The following have taught me much in their lectures, writings, homilies, and/or in consultation: Fr. Gerard Broccolo, Judy Bullock, Fr. Walter Burghardt, S.J., Fr. Jack Conley, C.P., Fr. Jim DeManuele, C.P., Fr. Chuck Faso, O.F.M., Fr. Bill Griner, Gabe Huck, Patricia Sanchez, Fr. Dennis Smolarski, S.J., and Fr. Eugene A. Walsh, S.S.

I would like to thank Mr. Jerry Seiden of *Spirit of Hope Publishing* for mentoring me through this book project, and for his diligent work in polishing and rewriting much of the text. Thanks also to Chelese Palmer for her editing work. I am very grateful to Mr. Joseph Roy of Tarrywood Designs for providing his beautiful art work. And I want to thank Mr. Steve Pulone for capturing the right mood on the cover photo and Mr. Anthony Montesione for the acton photo on the back cover.

Special thanks to Bishop Gabino Zavala for his inspiring *Foreword.*

FOREWORD

In the opening paragraph of his Apostolic Exhortation, *Sacramentum Caritatis*, Pope Benedict XVI observes, "What amazement must the Apostles have felt in witnessing what the Lord did and said during that (Last) Supper! What wonder must the Eucharistic mystery also awaken in our own hearts!"

It is with our hearts that we participate in the Holy sacrifice of Mass. But our participation does not end after an hour or so on Sunday morning. In *Our Hearts at Sunday Mass,* Fr. Alan explains how our participation involves our hearts all week long. On our journey of faith all our thoughts, words and actions flow from and lead to the Eucharistic celebration. We live out every day what we celebrate on the Lord's Day.

The Mass is a mystery that continually reveals itself to us as we grow in our faith. Fr. Alan presents a practical guide for the person in the pew looking for greater understanding of this mystery. His writing is clear. His approach is pastoral. This is a book for practicing Catholics to read over and over again. It is an invitation to reflect more deeply in the celebration in which they participate every Sunday of the year. It is a book to be given to those who have stopped going to church, or only go at Christmas and Easter. Teens will find in this book the inspiration they need to continue practicing their faith. Candidates in RCIA programs will enjoy learning about the attitudes that accompany our actions at Mass and non-Catholic spouses will come to understand how their husband or wife prays on Sunday.

This is a book that will bring joy to all who put its wisdom into practice.

Sincerely in Christ,

+ Gabino Zavala

Most Reverend Gabino Zavala, D.D., J.C.L.
Auxiliary Bishop
Archdiocese of Los Angeles

TABLE OF CONTENTS

Come, let us sing joyfully to the Lord;
cry out to the rock of our salvation.

Let us greet him with a song of praise,
joyfully sing out our psalms.

For the Lord is the great God,
the great king over all gods,

Whose hand holds the depths of the earth;
who owns the tops of the mountains.

—Psalm 95:1-4

Celebration for All

But you are a chosen race, a royal priesthood, a holy nation, a people of his own, so that you may announce the praise of him who called you out of darkness into his wonderful light. —1 Peter 2:9

$\mathcal{I}$ stood in the back of church and prepared myself to sing and walk down the aisle. Then someone in front lifted his voice to the congregation and said, "Let's all rise and greet our celebrant, Father Alan." I couldn't help but cringe.

The correct designation for the priest at Mass is "priest celebrant" or "the presider" or "the presiding priest." But that's not why I cringed. My reaction was disappointment for the people. The term "celebrant" is the descriptive term to identify *everyone* gathered for worship!

The people in the pews are not spectators. The sanctuary is not a theater. The congregation is not a passive audience. The priest is not an actor to be watched. He does not play a role or say lines. No. The people together with their priest celebrant enter into the Mass with full and conscious participation as a "royal priesthood."

The ordained priest leads, presides, orchestrates, and directs the celebrants in worship. I encourage people to be active in worship. I invite them to meet and greet others and sit up close to the altar. I urge them to respond in dialogue with the priest in word and song. I exhort them to watch, listen, and engage their hearts, minds, and bodies in this great act of worship.

A congregation that participates together with full, heart-felt, and Spirit inspired worship will have great things happen to them and through them.

> *Pope Benedict XVI urged all Catholics to celebrate the liturgy with devotion and live in a way that demonstrates their faith.* —Apostolic Exhortation *Sacramentum Caritatis*, "The Sacrament of Charity"

Outward Expression—Inward Faith

Our Sunday celebration through the liturgy is a visible expression, personal choice, and devotional demonstration of our faith. Our celebration of the liturgy is faith expressed, life lived, and our affirmation of hope for the week ahead.

We assemble with brothers and sisters in the faith to hear and receive inspiration from the Word of God. We remember and celebrate Christ's sacrifice on the cross and offer ourselves with Him to the Father. We open ourselves up to be transformed by the Holy Spirit. We ask for mercy for ourselves and all the departed. We beg for help for our world, our church, and everyone present. We celebrate and give thanks for the blessings of the past week and receive the Bread of Life in order to serve God and neighbor in the week ahead.

All these actions make the Sunday Mass the center, the high point, the source and summit of our Christian living from week to week—all year long. All our thoughts, words, and deeds lead up to and flow from our Sunday gathering with God and the family of God.

My Hope

My sincere hope and sacred goal for this book is to provide readers with a practical and pastoral understanding of what we celebrate in the Holy Sacrifice of the Mass. I hope these pages will help the ones who have not experienced their joyful role as celebrants. May they find new insight and understanding to live and demonstrate all week long the faith they professed on Sunday.

> *Mother Church earnestly desires that all the faithful should be led to that full, conscious, and active participation in liturgical celebrations which is demanded by the very nature of the liturgy.* — Constitution on the Sacred Liturgy, #14

AUTHOR'S NOTE: Use the "Personal Reflection" below, and at the end of every chapter, as you wish. But may I suggest that you use this space after you have reviewed each chapter and highlighted material for your thought. Take a moment to reflect on the key ideas and concepts. And use the space to 1) journal a summary of your thoughts, 2) list practical ways to live the lessons, and 3) note other insights or actions that surfaced.

Personal Reflection:

Preparing for Sunday Mass

The subtitle of this book is "Ten Steps to a Joyful Life." As you will read, the first two steps or attitudes involve our preparation for Sunday Mass. And then the other eight steps or attitudes relate to the five "rites" or parts of the Mass. Ten may seem like a lot to remember, much less to put into practice. Yet they are familiar attitudes to every Christian. I simply show how these attitudes manifest the life of Christ in us and lead us deeply into the experience of His joy.

This joy was first experienced by John the Baptist. We read in chapter one of Luke's gospel that Mary went to visit her cousin Elizabeth. Both women were pregnant. Mary entered the home and greeted her cousin, and Elizabeth was filled with the Holy Spirit. The baby within her leaped for joy! Yet unborn, John the Baptist was already stirred by the nearness of the Lord.

From the womb of Mary, Jesus brought blessing and jubilation to those near him. His adult life and ministry extended that same presence and power to countless others. That same blessing and nearness of Jesus is available today through the Word, Sacrament, and Community on Sunday morning.

Still, the ones expectant in spirit and open of heart receive a greater measure. They prepare and anticipate the presence of Jesus. They come to receive the One who instills joy, inspires hope, and enlivens our mortal bodies to leap, sing, praise, and express thanksgiving and adoration.

For those who have not experienced this joyful connection, don't despair. You are not alone. Read on. The following chapters offer insights and understanding to help open our hearts and focus our attitudes. May the Spirit of God guide us on this path to joy.

Personal Reflection:

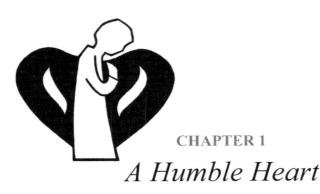

CHAPTER 1

A Humble Heart

Have you [Job] ever in your lifetime commanded the morning and shown the dawn its place? —Job 38:12

Humility Quotes

*J*am a collector of quotes. My personal treasury is full of words on humility—below are some of my favorites:

> *If you are all wrapped up in yourself, you are overdressed.* —Kate Halverson
>
> *A modest person is usually admired, if people ever hear of him.* —Edgar Watson Howe
>
> *I was humble for a while, but nobody noticed.* —Anonymous
>
> *After the game, the king and the pawn go back into the same box.* —Italian Proverb

St. Augustine made a comment on humility that is worthy of consideration. Every reading moves me to meditate, prods me to pause and ponder his thought. He said:

> *If you should ask me concerning the precepts, the laws, of the Christian faith, I should answer you, 'Nothing but humility.'*

Hmmm...

Humility is important, of course. Yet Augustine seems to say it is all we need!

Humility Is Truth

Humility is a real and honest relationship with the truth. For example, the truth is that we humans are small in the grand scheme of things.

How small?

Let's say I live to be a hundred years old. *Considered pretty old, right?* Yet scientists estimate the universe to be about fourteen billion years old! A hundred years of life is just a blip, a twinkling of the eye compared to the age of the stars.

I'm six feet four inches tall. *Considered pretty tall, right?* Yet next to Mount Everest I'm microscopic! Mount Everest is a tiny pebble compared to planet Earth. This globe we call home is a dot that orbits a small star in the vast Milky Way galaxy. And our great galaxy is just one of a hundred billion galaxies! *A hundred billion galaxies!*

In both time and size, we humans are like grains of sand in the Sahara Desert.

> *You have been told, O man, what is good, and what the Lord requires of you: Only to do right and to love goodness, and to walk humbly with your God.*
> —Micah 6:8

Humbled by God

The book of Job is known for tragedies, hardships, arguments, and complaints. Still, the final chapters of Job's story shine far brighter than the sorrows. The Lord comes in the storm and whirlwind to speak with Job. His awesome presence and divine declaration offered Job a true perspective on his small, short-sighted life.

God's message to and dialogue with Job continues to teach today. Anyone who reads and grasps the authority and truth of those words will be moved to humility, and agree with Job. He said:

> *I have dealt with great things that I do not understand, things too wonderful for me, which I cannot know.* —Job 42:3

Humility—based upon truth—reminds us of our minuscule measure before the infinite, eternal Master. Humility teaches our posture and place before the Almighty and all knowing God. Humility leads little creatures like us to bow our heads in worship and adoration before the Creator of this vast universe. And for St. Augustine that takes care of the first three commandments.

> *When I see your heavens, the work of your fingers, the moon and stars that you set in place, what are humans that you are mindful of them, mere mortals that you care for them?* —Psalm 8:4-5

The Truth about Us

Humility is truth. And the truth is that all of us are very talented and gifted. Yet the Apostle Paul's words are also true. He said, *What do you possess that you have not received* (1 Corinthians 4:7)? Everything we possess is a gift.

Our minds and bodies, our family and friends are all gifts from God. Our talents, abilities, knowledge, and wisdom all come from above. Our hope, courage, strength, daily bread, and every new dawn are all given by our heavenly Father. And our faith, forgiveness, and the promise of eternal life are gifts from the God of hope.

All that we have are gifts. What do good people say when they receive gifts? They say, *Thanks!* What do good people do with the gifts they receive? They *share!* And that takes care of a few other commandments.

Truth about Possessions

Humility is truth. And the truth is that all we possess is given to us. So we have no grounds to put anyone else down. The one faster, stronger, or smarter dare not boast, brag, or belittle others in false pride. The Lord who gave the gift can also take it away.

We are all made by the same Creator. Any prejudice against others because of color, nationality, or ethnic origin is both ignorant and absurd. Arrogance, bullying, insults, and discrimination cannot coexist with humility. And that should take care of a few more commandments.

Truth about Needs

Humility is truth. And the truth is, with all our gifts and talents, we still have many needs. We have sins that need forgiving. We have hurts that need healing. And we have weaknesses that need strengthening.

We all have physical, mental, emotional, relational, and financial needs. Experience and Scripture teach that without God we can do nothing. Psalm 127 declares, *Unless the Lord build the house, they labor in vain who build.* We are dependent creatures. We need to ask, seek, and knock for help.

> *The reward of humility and fear of the Lord is riches, honor and life.* —Proverbs 22:4

Truth about Ignorance

Humility is truth. And it is true that we are quite ignorant. We, the human family, have not learned to live in peace. We have not learned to feed the hungry of our world. We have not learned to respect and treasure all human life. We have only begun to learn how to care for our planet and its creatures.

Humility will admit ignorance. It leads us to beg for knowledge and wisdom. So humility touches on the precepts about prayers of petition.

Humility to Forgive

Humility is truth. And the truth is that at times we have all failed to follow God's laws.

The gospel of John, chapter eight, records the story of the woman caught in the act of adultery. The crowd was ready to stone her to death. But first they brought the woman to Jesus. "What do you think?" They asked him.

"Let the one among you who is without sin be the first to throw a stone at her," he answered.

No stones were thrown. *Why?* No one qualified.

We know all too well the faults and weaknesses that plague us. We have character to develop and virtues to cultivate. In short, we still have lots of growing up to do.

Humility reveals our limitations and needs. Humility reminds us of the weakness we share with others. Humility gives us patience and forgiveness, and it teaches us not to judge anyone. That takes care of a few more commandments.

Nothing but humility, Augustine said.

Humility….
- Makes us patient and forgiving—*Reconciliation*.
- Removes false pride and prejudice—*Gathering Rite.*
- Opens us up to learning—*Liturgy of the Word.*
- Moves us to ask and give thanks—*Eucharistic Prayer*.
- Helps us turn more of ourselves to God—*Communion.*
- Inspires us to share—*Rite of Dismissal.*

Humility that Worships

The recognition of our littleness and dependence prepares us for worship. We are ready to open our hands in prayer and ask for what we need. We are ready to lift our hands and give thanks for all we receive. And we are ready to reach out our hands to others—brothers and sisters, our equals in the sight of God. In other words, humility opens the way for our full, conscious, and active participation at Mass.

Carl Jung was asked, "Why do prayers to God frequently go unanswered today? God seemed more attentive to prayers in the past."

"When I hear such questions," Jung answered, "it always makes me think of the rabbi who was asked how it could be that God often showed himself to people in the olden days while nowadays nobody ever sees him. The rabbi replied, 'Nowadays, there is no longer anybody who can bow low enough.'"

In your relations with one another, clothe yourselves with humility, because God is stern with the arrogant but to the humble he shows kindness. —1 Peter 5:5

Humility to Be Free

Humility does not shroud our gifts or suppress our talents. Humility does not deny our abilities or demean our individuality. Humility does not make us invisible, inferior, or indifferent. And humility takes nothing from us except the lies that have limited our lives and vision.

Once we know the truth, we live in liberty. Humility frees us from the fear of being noticed. We are who we are. Humility frees us from the anxiety of performance. We do the best we can. Humility frees us from the stress of people pleasing. We no longer need the approval of others. Humility frees us from the need to control our world. We know the outcome is not in our power.

Humility frees us from the need to be right. We accept our limits. Humility frees us from the fluster we feel for well deserved praise. We used the gifts we were given. Humility frees us to be ourselves—at our best under all circumstances. We are who we are, sons and daughters made in the image of the One whose self-description is, "I Am."

> *You will know the truth, and the truth will set you free.* —John 8:32

Divine Humility

Imagine an ant and a twenty-foot-tall person. The ant wants to snuggle up to the person. But the ant finds it perilous and nigh impossible to get close to someone so big.

Now stretch your imagination. Picture a one-cell amoeba with desires to snuggle with a fifty-foot-tall person. But the tall person can't even see the microscopic admirer. Now imagine little you and me want to be friends of God. We feel insignificant and beyond microscopic next to the infinite, divine Being.

How can we possibly bond with God?

The Apostle Paul provides us with the answer. He wrote that Jesus...

> *...Emptied himself, taking the form of a slave, coming in human likeness; and found human in appearance, he humbled himself, becoming obedient to death, even death on a cross.* —Philippians 2:6-8

Jesus became one of us! Through baptism we became members of his body. So when he goes to the Father, he takes us with him.

Herein lies a great mystery. Our faith tells us that God so loved each minuscule, human person—us—that he sent his Son to become one of us. Then the Son, who loves us, lifts us up to the Father!

God doesn't hear our prayers because we shout loud or sing on key. God hears our prayers because we are baptized members of the Body of Christ. Our prayers are in Christ, with Christ, and through Christ. The Father hears his Son and all those joined to him. It is our union with Christ that makes our prayers at Mass so powerful.

A Position of Preparation

In the ordination ceremony for a priest, the one to be ordained lays prostrate before the altar for a period of prayer. At the start of Good Friday liturgy the priest lays prostrate before the altar for a few minutes of prayer. Physical prostration of the body is an act and attitude of humility before God. To prepare ourselves for Sunday Mass we might imagine ourselves prostrate before the throne of God. This image that begins in our minds will move our hearts, adjust our attitudes, empower our bodies, and engage our whole beings for the great act of worship!

This humble confidence is the foundation for meaningful worship and the first step to a joyful life.

Holiness is not in one exercise or another. It consists in a disposition of the heart, which renders us humble and little in the hands of God, conscious of our weakness but confident, even daringly confident, in his fatherly goodness. —St. Therese of Lisieux

Personal Reflection:

CHAPTER 2

A Forgiving Heart

*If you bring your gift to the altar, and there recall
that your brother or sister has anything against you,
leave your gift there at the altar, go first and be
reconciled with your brother or sister, and then come
and offer your gift.* —Matthew 5:23-24

Reconciliation Is Difficult

Go first and be reconciled.... This can be tough.
Reconciliation is difficult when a person caused us
deep and enduring pain. Reconciliation is difficult when
a person won't apologize. Reconciliation is difficult when
we'd rather get even. Reconciliation challenges the core
of our being.

*So how can we leave our gift at the altar and go make
things right?*

Reasons for Resentments

I have helped many wounded people come back to
the church. Some returned after five and ten years
away—others even longer. My ministry to and concern
for these people has given me insight and understanding.
I have learned that people fall away from the church for
a variety of reasons.

People have told me of the rubs, rifts, and resentments
that led to leaving. Some said they were hurt by a priest's

treatment in the confessional. Others were embarrassed and angered by the actions of a religious brother or nun in the classroom. Still others were upset by a pastor who bawled them out in front of friends.

I have also heard people share far more serious and ruinous reasons for leaving the church. Some have told me of pain caused by pedophilia and other profound abuse. These wounds pierce deeply and require special compassion and care.

But the harm felt and offense taken goes beyond issues with religious professionals. Today many of the laity are in leadership roles within our parishes. Some people have told me they were hurt by something the parish council president said. Or some felt they were treated unfairly by the school board. Others were slighted by the head of the choir. Parish leaders are not perfect. Not every leader is kind and just in every circumstance.

What about You?

So I can't help but wonder…among the readers of this book, are there some who are still hurt? Are there some who have not returned because of something a priest, deacon, brother, nun, teacher, lay parish leader once said or did? Are there some readers who waited for an apology that never came? Have some moved away without any resolution—only separation? Have some died while distant? Readers, are any of you still hurting?

I speak to you as a priest, a representative of the official church and all its leaders. I offer sincere apologies to all of you who have been unjustly treated by church personnel. On behalf of the church, I say, **"We are sorry."**

Like the people we serve, church leaders are human beings, too. We all have feet of clay. We have bad days. We make mistakes. We say the wrong things. We have our share of faults, failings, and limitations. We do stupid things, and to sin is the most stupid. We are sorry, and we ask for your understanding and your forgiveness.

The Other Side
Of course, it works both ways. I have endured hurt from some of the people I served. I have been insulted, ignored, misunderstood, and unappreciated. And I know other church leaders who have had similar experiences.

Among the readers of this book, there are some who have hurt a church leader. Some know they caused harm to one of us. So I can't help but wonder, again. Are you absent from us because of the hurt or harm you caused? Are you afraid to return because of your words or actions? Have you separated yourself and can't bring yourself to bridge the gap and return?

I appeal to you, again. As a priest and one in a position of church leadership, I make this declaration. For any and all hurt you caused us, we in church leadership say, **"We forgive you."** For any harm you have done to us, "We forgive you." For any insults, injuries, offenses— real or perceived, "We forgive you." We put the past behind us and we desire to be completely reconciled with all.

The Bigger Picture
I'd like to expand the picture, now. Every community is made up of families. And families consist of relationships between parents, children, grandparents, siblings, in-laws, and so on. Love binds family together, right?

Yet, no matter how great the love, parents say and do things that hurt children. Perhaps an unkind word was spoken, a promise was not kept, or a bad example was set. Maybe a commitment was neglected, a lie was told, or private space was invaded.

Children, filled with love for parents, can also cause them hurt and bring them harm. Perhaps tempers flared and harsh words were spoken. Or parents were disobeyed and their rules disregarded. Maybe chores or household needs were neglected. Or there were struggles, strife, stress, and scraps among siblings.

Husbands and wives founded their union on love. Still, harm and hurts inflicted damage and caused distance. Perhaps insensitive words were spoken. Perhaps there were injuries imposed, offense taken, and feelings bruised. Maybe a spouse was overly demanding. Or there were unreasonable expectations, rigid requirements, or unexplained periods of absence—emotional and otherwise.

Families with great love, faith, commitment, and Christian character still face strife and struggles. Things go wrong, hurts happen, harm is done.

Today and everyday is a good day to express a heartfelt, **"I'm sorry."**

To the Innocent

Still, some people say they did no harm—no hurt. They were the ones picked on, mistreated, ignored, or unappreciated. At first they were angry and upset. But in time and with water under the bridge, now might be the moment to act.

Today and every day is a good time to stand tall and speak those beautiful words, **"I forgive you."** And it might help to add, "I'm not perfect either. I remember the times you forgave me. Let's start over."

We are thankful for reconciliation. What a peaceful feeling!

Words that Bond

Reconciliation and healing happens when there is honest apology, "I'm sorry," accompanied with true pardon, "I forgive you." These two short sentences bond us together into a strong, understanding, patient, and united people. That's why I state that the second habit of highly joyful people is reconciliation.

Reconciliation frees up both the offenders and the offended. The past is healed and each is able to enter the future released of guilty feelings and the desire for revenge.

Reconciliation removes the resentment we harbored for those who harmed and offended us. It releases the unwillingness to forgive that muted our prayers. God's ears are no longer deaf to our plea for mercy. And we are ready and able to say those daring words, "Father…forgive us our trespasses, as we forgive those who trespass against us."

Reconciliation makes room in our hearts for good feelings. It makes us ready to join the assembled people and celebrate the Eucharist.

The Sacrament of Reconciliation

The Catholic Church has a beautiful sacrament that we call "Reconciliation."

Reconciliation is a big word. How many syllables? Six. We sometimes call this sacrament "Confession." That's a three syllable word. We also sometimes refer to this sacrament as "Penance." That's two syllables. I like one syllable words. So I refer to this great sacrament as God's "hug."

That's not original with me. That was Jesus' message in the story of the prodigal son. What did the father in the story do? Before the returning son could express his sorrow or ask forgiveness, the father sprung into action. He ran to his son, put his arms around him, and gave him a great big hug. In this story, Jesus was saying, "This is an image of my Father. This is how my Father loves you." (See Luke 15:11-32).

Calvary's Convert
Remember the convert on Calvary? It was one of the centurions. In the gospel of Mark we read:

When the centurion who stood facing him [Jesus] saw how he breathed his last he said, 'Truly this man was the Son of God!' —Mark 15:39

What did the centurion see? He had seen many men die on a cross. That was nothing new. He had not seen a crucified man do what Jesus did. In the agony and grip of death, Jesus cried out, *Father, forgive them for they know not what they do* (Luke 23:34). The centurion witnessed the manner of Jesus' death and his manner of forgiveness. Seeing this, the centurion became a believer.

People are still drawn to Christ when they see us forgive. Many are hungry for a genuine forgiving community. We, Christ's followers, are still on display before the eyes of a world hungry for mercy.

Honest Recall to Forgive
Forgiveness starts with self-knowledge. We look down at our feet of clay and remember that we are less than perfect. We recall the times we stood in need of forgiveness. We recall the offenses we caused. The realization of our less-than-perfect past prompts us to extend understanding to others.

In fact, imperfect people are all we have here on earth. *How can imperfect people make life's journey a workable experience?* By the constant use of those two sentences, "I'm sorry," and "I forgive." With these two sentences weaving in and out of our relationships, we have a beautiful and durable fabric of family and community.

*A happy marriage is the union of
two good forgivers.* —Robert Quillen

Making Lists

One day a husband and wife were arguing.

She complained, "You're late again. Why don't you get home on time once in a while?"

He shouted back, "This place is such a mess. What did you do all day?"

Then she got him with, "And when are you going to cut the grass. It's so high it's an embarrassment."

He retorted, "Nag, nag, nag. I've had a difficult day. Can't I have a little peace when I get home?"

The wife opened her mouth to reply, but her husband held up his hand. He said, "Hold it. We've been griping at each other all week long. Here, let's take a piece of paper and write down our complaints. Then we can calmly go through them, one by one, and rationally try to solve them."

The wife agreed. So they sat down at the kitchen table. After a bit of reflection, the wife started her list. And shortly after, the husband started writing.

"No more than twenty items," the wife said. She felt a bit calmer.

After a few minutes, they both stopped writing. The husband said, "Okay, I'm ready. Let me see your list."

"No," the wife said, "This was your idea. I want to see your list first."

"Well, all right," the husband agreed. And he handed her his list. It was numbered from one to twenty.

She read it. Twenty times down the page he wrote, "I love you, Jenny." "I love you, Jenny."

A couple of tears began to trickle down her cheek. She looked up, gently smiled and said, "I'm sorry, I…"

He jumped in, "Yes, I'm sorry, too."

She crumpled up her list. They hugged. Both had tears. And both had smiles that came from deep within. It became an evening of good memories, warm feelings, and renewed hope.

Here Come Da Judge—Not

Let's change the scene a bit.

It's just you, the reader, now. Imagine yourself alone and quiet at the kitchen table. Picture yourself in preparation before you go to the Sacrament of Reconciliation.

You pray. You tell God that you are sorry for your sins. You examine your conscience. You remember the sins since your last confession. To make sure you don't go blank when you see the priest, you jot down words to jog your memory. You write: dishonesty, harsh words, selfishness, laziness, etc.

Your list starts to get a bit long. You hear a sound and are shocked to see the Lord Jesus. He's at the other end of the table deep in thought. And he's writing, too.

Your shock turns to anxiety and concern. You worry, "Oh, no. God knows everything. All secret sins and shameful things are an open book to the Lord. I've pictured him as that stern and fearful judge high above with my file full of my every fault." Then you wonder, "What will he say about my list?"

The Lord Jesus stops writing and lifts his head. His eyes meet yours. He motions and reaches out. He wants to read your list of sins. You give him the list and watch and wonder as he glances over it.

Then he hands you his sheet of paper. You look at it and read. It is numbered from one to twenty. You read every line. The Lord wrote over and over, "I love you, John." "I love you, John." And in the final line he added, "Always have. Always will."

Joy In Heaven

Okay, it's just a story. But remember what Jesus told us:

> *There will be more joy in heaven over one sinner who repents than over ninety-nine righteous people who have no need of repentance.* —Luke 15:7

One interpreter reflected that the ninety-nine are the multitudes of angels and archangels, principalities and powers, gathered around God's throne in heaven. The one lost sheep is us, the human race on earth. God so loved the world, *us,* that He asked his Son to leave heaven for a while and go down to earth. He asked him to teach us, lead us to sorrow, forgive us, die on the cross for us, and so reconcile and save us. Then there will be great rejoicing!

The Bishop's Secret

There was a visionary who lived many years ago. The local bishop heard that someone in his diocese was having visions of Jesus, and he was very skeptical. He found out who she was and asked her to come see him.

The visionary arrived, and the bishop said, "It is my responsibility to investigate the authenticity of any miraculous events or happenings within the diocese. And your visions have been reported to me. Would you be willing to cooperate?"

The visionary nodded and agreed.

The bishop said, "Then, I have some instructions for you. The next time Jesus appears to you, I'd like you to ask him two questions. First ask him, 'When did the bishop last go to confession?' And second ask him, 'What did he confess?'

"Because of the seal of confession," the bishop said to himself, "no one will ever know what I confessed."

A week or two went by and the visionary returned. The bishop asked her, "Did you see Jesus this week?"

"Yes," she answered.

"And did you ask him when I last went to confession?"

"Yes, and Jesus told me that you went to confession at the Benedictine monastery twelve days ago."

The bishop was startled. She was right about the place and number of days. A little unsettled, he asked, "And did you ask Jesus what I confessed."

"Yes," she said, and then paused.

"Well....?" the bishop probed.

The visionary's countenance seemed to change. Her face was warm and her voice was soft. She answered, "Jesus said he forgot."

God's Eraser

The parables of Jesus tell us about God. They tell us how much God cares and wants all the lost to be found. They illustrate his hunger for all sinners to be reconciled. They demonstrate the divine desire for all people to be back at home in God's heart. Our God has a big eraser.

Before we celebrate Mass, we need to be reconciled with God and with one another. Reconciliation opens our hearts to receive inner wholeness, experience true community, and receive the gift of inner peace that surpasses all understanding. Reconciliation is the second step to a joyful life.

Personal Reflection:

The Gathering Rite

The Mass like any multi-faceted experience has parts and elements that make the whole. Each element is important to understand and appreciate for the Mass experience to be special in the heart of the worshipper. The following chapter has to do with the attitude we bring to the beginning of Mass. This is the first of eight reflections related to five parts or "rites" of the Mass.

The **Gathering Rite** begins when we set foot on the church property. It involves meeting and greeting people as we approach the church.

Then once inside it continues with:

- The Entrance Song
- Greeting
- Act of Penitence and/or Kyrie
- Gloria
- Opening Prayer

CHAPTER 3

A Welcoming Heart

Do not neglect hospitality, for through it some have unknowingly entertained angels. —Hebrews 13:2

One Missing Thing

What do you consider the most important part of a good meal?

Most people look forward to a great entrée, like steak or lobster. Some look for lots of healthy garden-fresh vegetables steamed to perfection. Others are the soup people who want rich broth with chunks of meat, veggies and home-style noodles. There are some who hunger for a big salad with a variety of fresh ingredients and perfect dressing. And of course, others are all about dessert—decadent multi-layered cake, exotic cream filled delights, or hot apple pie with ice cream.

Now with mouth watering and stomach growling, imagine something for me. Picture yourself out for a good meal. You're about to enjoy everything imagined above plus a choice wine and the finest gourmet coffee. And in the background, a great band plays your favorite music. Everything is perfect, except....

There is one thing that's absent. One missed item leaves you empty, waiting, and wanting. All the good food, drink, music, and atmosphere can't fill that small empty space. And you know that there is one item needed to complete the experience.

No one extended warmth and welcome to you. No one acknowledged your arrival or presence. No one talked to you before, during, or after the meal. No one seemed to notice or even care that you were there. No one smiled or connected with you in any way. The only person who didn't ignore you was the person who wanted the money.

The best food, drink, music, and surroundings were not enough. It was not an enjoyable meal for you. In fact, it was a very lonely experience. You did not feel like you belonged. There was no warmth, no hospitality.

Some people say that's how they feel at Sunday Mass. They come to participate in a sacred meal and partake in the Lord's Banquet. Yet among the Lord's people, there is no warmth or welcome. They find that no one greets them, no one smiles, no one shakes their hand, no one calls them by name, no one notices their presence— except at collection time. They feel like outsiders, strangers, and aliens who don't belong. And they leave feeling that no one cared that they came.

Encounter with Loneliness

A few years ago, I had some time off for study. That meant that I didn't have to preside at Sunday Eucharist. Instead, I could sit in the pews and participate with the people.

I visited as many churches as I could. I wanted a variety of experiences. I wondered how I would be greeted and welcomed at other churches. And I attended thirty churches!

I'm not difficult to see. My six feet four inches gives me visibility. Still, only at three of the churches did anyone speak to me, welcome me, or notice me. At the other twenty-seven churches, I was a stranger.

At ninety percent of the churches, no one spoke to me. No one greeted me at the door before Mass. No one said, "Good-bye" afterward. The only words to me were at the formal *Greeting of Peace* rite.

Still, it disappointed me—so many Sunday mornings without warmth, welcome, or notice. Over and over, my Banquet of the Lord was an encounter with loneliness.

What If the One Ignored....

I didn't take it personally. I wasn't ignored on purpose. No one knew that I was a priest—no black suit and clerical collar. People were wrapped up in their own affairs. They were focused on their own family, friends, and folks they already knew. Some may have had a fear of strangers.

On the other hand, not many visitors or guests are like me. The majority of the ones ignored have special circumstances and unique needs that brought them to church. They carry burdens, expectations, and hopes in with them.

What if the one ignored was one of the following?

- A wounded soul who had come to church after a ten or twenty year absence.
- A newcomer looking for a church to join.
- Someone who had just lost a loved one and was in need of warmth, comfort, and support.
- An addict who decided to ask for help from a church community.
- A confused and empty teenager with thoughts of never returning to church.
- An abused spouse or young person in need of courage to seek help.
- Or a host of others with a variety of troubles.

Who knows what hurts are ignored with each person? We will never know how many people no longer come to church today because no one welcomed them.

There are basics needs that we all have. We need to belong and feel like we're a part of a group. We need to be noticed, honored, and respected. We all hunger for a warm welcome, an inviting smile, and a firm handshake. Acts of friendship and kindness can do wonders and build up a community of faith.

Remember the ideal meal? Apply this experience to Sunday Mass. The lector proclaims the Word well. The homily is on target. The musicians and singers are in tune. The Eucharistic ministers and altar servers all do well. Everything can be at its best, but without a warm welcome, Mass can still leave someone feeling empty and negative. Without a spirit of friendliness and hospitality, some will leave in need and in loneliness.

Important Business

I recently went to a car rental office. From the moment I entered, the staff made me feel like an important person. They greeted me with smiles. They called me by name. They were concerned to meet my needs and they wanted to make me happy. They succeeded!

Good businesses know how important it is to make customers feel significant. They know how to be warm and friendly. They want to meet the customers' needs.

How much more is it the business of God's people to make His flock feel welcome and wanted? We have more at stake than profits. We have God's people to meet and greet on Sunday morning. We have the joyful privilege to make each other feel significant and valued.

Next to the Blessed Sacrament itself, your neighbor is the holiest object present to your senses. — C. S. Lewis

Sacred Places

Gaze around any Catholic church and you'll see lots of sacred places. For instance, the tabernacle is a very sacred place. When the sanctuary lamp is burning we know that the Blessed Sacrament is present. When we walk past the tabernacle, we genuflect to our Lord.

The altar is also a very sacred place. It is here that the Eucharistic Prayer is proclaimed by the priest, and the bread and wine become the Body and Blood of Christ. Our souls are nourished from this holy altar at Communion time.

The ambo is a very sacred place. From here the Word of God is proclaimed. And we are given constant assurance of God's love.

The baptistery is very sacred. This is the place where our life of faith begins. We become members of the Body of Christ in the waters and wonders of baptism.

The reconciliation room or confessional is a sacred place. It is here that God's mercy is lavished upon us, and we are given the renewed assurance of forgiveness.

So what is the most sacred place in our churches?

The most sacred place in our churches is **wherever you and I are**. St. Paul declares:

> *Do you not know that you are a temple of God, and that the Spirit of God dwells in you? For the temple of God, which you are, is holy.* —1 Corinthians 3:16-17

I enter a Catholic church and genuflect to our Lord present in the tabernacle. But I could just as well turn to the assembled people and genuflect to the Lord present in all of them.

A tabernacle may be decorated with gold and precious stones. But it is still just a material thing. It has no life. You and I are living temples of God. We have minds that can know truth, wills that can choose good, hands that can serve and hearts that can love. What a masterpiece of creation and grace we are.

So our attitude of hospitality begins with awe and wonder for all human persons. And that includes the one we see in the mirror.

The Hospitality of God

An attitude of hospitality may seem like a nice virtue or good manners, but it is much more than that. It touches on how we envision God. It changes how we proclaim God. And it adjusts how we imitate God.

What does Psalm 23 say about God?

- *In green pastures you let me graze...*
- *To safe waters you lead me...*
- *You are at my side...*
- *You set a table before me...*
- *You anoint my head with oil...*
- *My cup overflows...*
- *I will dwell in the house of the Lord....*

Hospitality is God's middle name!

In the gospels we see Jesus multiplying loaves and fishes. He satisfied the physical hunger of the crowds that followed him. After the resurrection, he's on the seashore cooking breakfast for his apostles. But more importantly, he hosts the Last Supper. He gives his apostles, and us, his Body and Blood as food and drink. Jesus feeds us and nourishes with both his teaching and the Sacrament of the Holy Eucharist. The Holy Mass is God's great act of hospitality.

Kindness Matters

In the Judeo-Christian tradition, we have a story about the first sin. In the Garden of Eden, Adam and Eve disobeyed God and rebelled by eating forbidden fruit.

The consequence? They and all those after them experienced hard work, suffering, sickness and death.

The Maasai tribe in Africa has a different story. Theirs is not about forbidden fruit in a garden but about a good time around a campfire. Amid the food and festivity a stranger came to them. He asked for hospitality—a place to stay and food to eat. The ancestors turned him away. They couldn't be bothered. Their behavior was inhospitable, unkind, and unlike God. They were punished with lives of hard work, suffering, sickness and death.

Abraham and Sarah had a spirit of hospitality. In the book of Genesis, three travelers stopped by their home. Abraham greeted them, bowed down, and sought to meet their needs. He said:

> *Let some water be brought, that you may bathe your feet, and then rest yourselves under the tree... Let me bring you a little food that you may refresh yourselves.*

Abraham and Sarah went all out to provide hospitality, refreshment, and honor. *The consequence?* The couple received their hearts' desire. A year later they were given the gift of a child. (See Genesis 18:1-15).

A similar story about a Shunammite woman is in the book of 2nd Kings. She showed great hospitality to the prophet Elisha. She fed him on many occasions. She even built a chamber for the prophet upstairs in her house. The consequence? This gracious yet barren woman was granted her desire to bear a child (see 2 Kings 4: 8-17).

Two Feet beyond Hospitality

Abraham and Sarah made sure the visitors could bathe their feet. In one gospel story, a woman washed Jesus' feet with her tears and dried them with her hair. At the last supper, Jesus washed the disciples' feet.

Those of us with material blessings can share our money, food, clothes, and goods with the needy. But to wash their feet changes the picture. It puts us at their level. Indeed, it puts us lower, at the level of servant. That's what Jesus did and asks us to do.

Hospitality—God's Measure

In Luke's gospel, Jesus tells us to love God with all our hearts and to love our neighbor as ourselves. But Jesus is asked, "Who is my neighbor?" He answers with the story of the Good Samaritan. What did the Good Samaritan do? He cared for the immediate needs of a stranger in need along the side of the road. He nursed his wounds, gave him food, took him to safety, and provided lodging. The Samaritan showed the stranger hospitality.

Why is this story so important?

Jesus identifies himself with the poor and needy. And in Matthew's gospel, the Lord makes that very clear. Jesus describes the last judgment scene of those who will be saved. He says that the Son of Man will be seated on his throne with all the nations assembled before him. To those on his right, he will say:

> *Inherit the kingdom prepared for you from the foundation of the world. For I was hungry and you gave me food, I was thirsty and you gave me drink, a stranger and you welcomed me.... Whatever you did for one of the least of my people, you did for me.*

Those on the Lord's left did not give him food when he was hungry. They did not give him drink when he was thirsty. They did not welcome him when he was a stranger. They did none of the kindnesses of the others. To them he will say, *Depart from me* (See Matthew 25: 31-46).

Hospitality is the standard by which we will be judged. *We will be shown what we have sown.*

Hospitality Is God's Nature

Scripture affirms that God is serious about hospitality. To be hospitable is to reflect the image and likeness of our loving God.

God the Father is our Creator and our Provider. He gives us the gifts of food, drink, clothing, shelter, and all good gifts from the earth. And the Father so loves us that he gives us his only Son, Jesus, to be our Savior and Redeemer.

Jesus lavishes us with his truth and mercy. He gives his life for us. He so loves us that He sends forth his Spirit, the Sanctifier, Counselor, and Comforter.

The Holy Spirit so loves us that he empowers us and endows us with gifts. He gives us spiritual gifts of wisdom, insight, leadership, power, courage, love, and more.

Yes, the Holy Trinity is all about giving. To give, to care, to share is at the very center of God's nature.

Love one another with mutual affection;
Anticipate one another in showing honor.
—Romans 12:10

A Family Resemblance?

If a first-time visitor to a Catholic church were to ask me, "Who are these people in church?" I would respond, "These people are, by baptism, brothers and sisters of the Lord Jesus. They are the family of God."

Chances are the visitor would look around and then ask, "Brothers and sisters? Family? Why are they sitting so far apart from each other? Don't they like each other?"

I can't help but wonder...

● What does our manner of gathering at Mass say about us?

● Does our group behavior show that we are a community?

● Does it demonstrate support for one another in prayer and personal concern?

● Do we meet and greet one another as a family does?

● Do we look into each others faces, know each other's names, and listen to each other's voices in prayer and song?

● Do we sense a feeling of belonging at Mass?

● Do visitors feel welcome and a part of us?

A Family Gathering

Compare how we gather for our Sacred Meal to the way we gather for Thanksgiving dinner at Grandma's.

In the Constitution on the Sacred Liturgy #26 from we read:

> *Liturgical services are not private functions, but are celebrations of the Church, the holy people....*

Many have grown up with the attitude that Mass is a "me and God" experience. We want our private encounter with the Lord. However, Sunday Mass is designed to be a "we and God" experience.

Almost all of our prayers at Mass are "we" prayers. "*We* ask this...." "Lord, hear *our* prayer." "Let *us* give thanks...." "*Our* Father...."

An individual seated alone and away from the gathered assembly on Sunday is like someone eating Thanksgiving dinner all alone in the basement or garage. All the family is gathered, but one is disconnected.

There are many opportunities throughout the week for our personal prayers. Sunday Mass is the time to expand our hearts and pray as one family with one voice as the people of God.

Any appearance of individualism or division among the faithful should be avoided, since we are all brothers and sisters in the sight of the one Father. —General Instruction on the Roman Missal, #62

People Friendly Spaces

Architecture has a great affect on how welcome people feel. Physical accommodations and personal considerations make the experience a pleasure or a pain. Here is a helpful checklist to consider:

- Is there a spacious gathering area in our church where people can meet and greet before Mass?
- Is there a space where refreshments can be served after Mass?
- Is there a guarded space in the vestibule where people can place their hats, coats, umbrellas, etc?
- Are there washrooms easily available?
- Is the building accessible and comfortable to the physically challenged?
- Are their greeters specially assigned to make sure all are welcomed in?
- Is the church environment warm and inviting? Is it tastefully decorated?
- Are there hymnals available for all?
- Is the music easy to sing, even for visitors?
- Is the speaking system adequate so all can hear?
- Do we have people signing for those who have lost their hearing?

A well planned gathering area can build a greater sense of community.

For instance, photos help people to relate to others. If there is a wall display full of pictures of the newly baptized, graduated, married, deceased, and so on, this helps a parish family put names and faces to news. The

Sunday bulletin should be abundant with photos of parishioners as well. Bulletin pictures grow a sense of community.

Names tags are a good idea. When the ministers of hospitality, lectors, extraordinary ministers of the Eucharist, acolytes, and those in music ministry wear name tags, people can easily identify those who serve them.

Hospitality During the Week

Hospitality can be many things. It's the offer to pick up people who are otherwise unable to get to church. It's an invitation to a neighbor or family member to come with us to church.

Hospitality always involves good manners. It always involves respectful language. It always involves smiles. It always involves behavior that acknowledges the dignity and worth of each individual we encounter.

Hospitality may involve the gift of things: food, clothing, shelter. What if we are poor and have nothing to give? Hospitality always involves the gift of attitudes. And everyone can give these:

● An attitude of welcome says in word and deed, "You are important. We like you. We want to spend time with you."

● An attitude of unconditional regard shows, "We don't judge you. We accept you as you are."

● An attitude of respect portrays, "You are a real person to us. Your thoughts and feelings are important to us."

● An attitude of patience and forgiveness says, "We are sorry if we have hurt you. We forgive you of any wrongs." This is at the core of world hospitality— living in peace on this planet.

● An attitude of understanding expresses, "We know what you must be going through. We understand your fears and worry. We understand your joy and laughter. We understand your tears and sorrow. And we value your hopes and dreams."

Hospitality is the response of readiness and affection that we express in the song *Here I am, Lord* (words and music by Dan Schutte, S.J. ©1981).

I will go Lord...
I will hold your people
in my heart.

Difficult Hospitality

All the attitudes of hospitality depend upon our ability to listen. The gospel of Luke (Chapter 10) tells of two women who provided hospitality to Jesus. Martha was in the kitchen—busy with chores. Mary was at the feet of Jesus—focused on the Lord.

Martha became upset with her sister Mary. She was not helping her. Still, the lesson is that both provided hospitality. One was active and laboring, the other attentive and listening.

We seldom think of listening as an act of hospitality. In fact, it is the most difficult act of hospitality. It is important to offer food, drink, shelter, and lodging to the distant or displaced from home. But it is also important to offer attention and affirmation to the person.

To offer the gift of hospitality by listening will awaken the ears of our soul to the voice of God. Open ears and heart are able to hear God speak within us. And what we hear will amaze us.

Obstacles to Hospitality

Many obstacles hinder hospitality. Prejudice is a barrier—in any form. Anger and the lack of forgiveness block our way. Narrow attitudes about appearance, apparel, or style bridle hospitality. Negative bias toward tattoos, far-out hair cuts, and body art blind a willing spirit.

Fear is a formidable force that hinders hospitality. Perhaps we are afraid to greet someone we gossiped about. We might fear rejection or disapproval from others. We might fear contact with those who seem rigid or cold. Or maybe we are "quiet types" and avoid people we don't know.

All obstacles to hospitality are a challenge for us to grow. Our entry into church and first glimpse of the tabernacle is our reminder. Every person gathered before Mass is a living tabernacle before whom we could genuflect. God dwells within them.

Brothers and Sisters

One day a beggar approached the Russian author Fyodor Dostoyevsky and asked him for some money. Dostoyevsky reached first in one pocket and then in another and came up empty-handed.

"I'm sorry, my brother, but I seemed to have left my wallet at home. I have nothing to give you."

The beggar looked at the famous man and smiled. "Oh, you've given me a lot, sir. You called me 'brother'."

The spirit of hospitality is rooted in the awareness that we are all brothers and sisters. We have the same heavenly Father. We are one family.

Rewards of Hospitality

What will be our reward for showing hospitality? We may seek the reward of a child, as Abraham and Sarah did. We may need better health. We may desire a relationship healed. We may need financial help. But the ultimate reward of hospitality is that God comes and dwells in us.

On Sunday morning we gather as a diverse people, young and old, rich and poor, sick and healthy, etc. We gather as a people of faith around the table of the Lord.

Our words, our smiles, and our many voices united as one make us feel like the family of God. Right from the beginning of Mass we know that somehow Jesus is present.

> *Whoever loves me will keep my word, and my Father will love him, and we will come to him and make our dwelling with him.* —John 14:23

Our hope is that this welcoming spirit, this spirit of unity and belonging of the **Gathering Rite** continues all throughout the week, so that we always experience Jesus in our midst. It is through hospitality that we get to know the heart of God. We gain a foretaste of the overflowing joy that will be ours at the heavenly banquet.

Personal Reflection:

The Liturgy of the Word

The **Liturgy of the Word** rite includes the following:

- Old Testament Reading
- Responsorial Psalm
- New Testament Reading
- Gospel Acclamation
- Gospel
- Homily
- Profession of Faith
- Prayer of the Faithful

CHAPTER 4

A Listening Heart

This is my beloved Son. Listen to him.
—Mark 9:7

A priest was in the market for a telescope. He entered the shop and picked up the first telescope that caught his eye. He looked through it—then put it down. He picked up another one. He looked through it—then put it down. He picked up one after the other—but nothing.

The priest would have picked up and peered through every telescope in the shop. But the clerk interrupted him.

"Excuse me—Father...." the clerk began. "Why don't you just ask your congregation to sit up closer?"

Brothers and Sisters

I encourage the congregation to sit up closer at Mass. They rarely do. I don't take it personally. Still, it is difficult to preach and proclaim the Word to someone a hundred feet away!

It's not just about me. I'm concerned for them. It is difficult for them to truly hear what is said. Hearing involves our ears, our eyes, our minds, our emotions, and our hearts.

Some years ago I went to see the musical, *1776*. The play focused on the people who founded the United States. I had a seat in the balcony. It was quite a distance from the stage. The whole play and performance was ho-hum for me.

Then some time later, I saw the same play again. I was at a dinner playhouse. I had a seat very close to the stage. What a difference! This time I enjoyed the experience.

Why the difference? I sat up close at the dinner playhouse. I *heard* in the fullest sense of that word. I heard all the words. I saw the actors act. I got the facial expressions. I caught the subtle emotions. I observed the convictions they portrayed. The characters and story came to life. I heard the play with my ears, my eyes, my mind, my emotions, and my heart.

I suspect that our up-close audience helped the actors, too. Our attention and excitement seemed to inspire and energize the actors to perform better. The sense of our close connection made them want to do their best.

Total Being Tuned-In

The advantages and enhanced experiences I had from a closer connection with a play also applies to Sunday Mass. The Lector may present the readings with great accuracy, understanding, and enthusiasm. But at fifty pews away.... It's difficult for people to participate at that distance. It's hard to catch the spirit and experience so far afield.

To sit alone is a problem, too. An audience listens as a body. We join together in attention, distraction, and reaction to the shared experience. And our reactions and responses affect those around us. Helen Hayes observed, "The audience is half the play."

This is true of the congregation during the **Liturgy of the Word**. The experience is enhanced near the front in the midst of others. Together we tune our ears, focus our eyes, direct our minds, engage our emotions, and open our hearts to receive. We benefit, but God's Word is honored. And we show respect for the person of faith who proclaims that Word.

Participation in the Liturgy of the Word involves our total being. Just hearing with ears falls short. Otherwise, closed eyes and an audio-recording of the readings would do. Or a quiet reading of the Scriptures by ourselves would suffice.

Instead, we gather to experience God's message. We come to know the Word of Scripture. We participate to connect with the living word—the person before us proclaiming his or her faith.

> *The Church has always venerated the divine scriptures just as she venerates the body of the Lord, since from the table of both the word of God and the body of Christ she unceasingly receives and offers to the faithful the bread of life.* —Constitution on Divine Revelation

Fulfilled Today

Luke's gospel records a visit Jesus made to the synagogue in Nazareth. He stood up to read and was handed the scroll of the prophet Isaiah, written centuries earlier. Jesus read the text and proclaimed, *Today this scripture passage is fulfilled in your hearing* (see Luke 4:16-21).

That is the key to our connection to Scripture on Sunday morning. And here is the question: How is what we hear fulfilled in our midst, right now?

Scripture is not a collection of books about history. Scripture is focused on the God of all history. Scripture is not a lesson on what happened two thousand years ago. Scripture is our guide to the mystery of salvation—accomplished yet available in our day.

For example, we know that Jesus healed the blind, the deaf, and the crippled two thousand years ago. But Jesus heals today. He opens up eyes blinded by prejudice. He heals ears that have been deaf to the cries of the poor. Jesus cures those who have been crippled by fear.

The proclamation of Scripture and the homily reveals to us that Jesus is alive and in our midst here and now. That message gives us understanding of God's saving action and transforming power that changes us today. And so we are prepared and led into Eucharist with thanksgiving and praise.

Keep Listening

Let's say that we take all this to heart and practice it on Sunday morning. We sit up front, tune our senses, focus our mind, and get involved. We listen with our hearts and truly benefit from the Scripture and homily at Mass.

Still, remember that humility is truth. And the truth is that God's Word is eternal, but our memories are not. St. Paul said, *We hold this treasure in earthen vessels...* (2 Corinthians 4:7). And the truth is that clay pots and people leak!

We need to hear God's Word outside of Mass and all week long. How do we listen to God in those other times?

Regular study and reflection upon Sacred Scripture. First of all, we take time to study both the Old Testament and the New Testament.

Notice that I said "study." The Bible can be difficult to understand. To merely read the Bible may confuse some. That's why many parishes have Bible study courses.

There are many books and online resources that offer in-depth information and Bible study aids. There are materials to understand the formation of Sacred Scripture. There are guides that provide the historical settings and the authors' intentions and purpose. Experts give us insights into the literary forms and the meanings of various ancient expressions and figures of speech.

On Monday read the Scripture passages for the following Sunday's Mass. This gives us a few days to wrestle with the text. We can research the parts we don't grasp. We have the opportunity to discuss the passages with our family and friends. And we have content for prayerful meditation throughout the week.

Studying the Bible is a necessary part of our lives—like eating and sleeping. As St. Jerome said, "To be ignorant of Scripture is to not know Christ."

Nature is another way to listen to God. It is not Scripture. Yet Scripture say that creation declares God's glory and sings His praises (see Psalm 19:1-6).

In the Broadway play, *My Fair Lady*, Eliza Doolittle sings to Freddie,

Sing me no song! Read me no rhyme!
Don't waste my time, Show me!
Don't talk of June, Don't talk of fall!
Don't talk at all! Show me!

The young lady wanted more than words about love. She wanted actions that made the words believable. She wanted a demonstration of affection.

Despite all our words, the experts say that human communication is 85% non-verbal. Our facial expressions, body language, and actions speak louder than our words. A funeral is a good example. We express sympathy with our words. But we convey our feelings with hugs, tears, gifts of flowers, and acts of kindness and support.

Nature is the living,
visible garment of God.
—Goethe

It's true that "actions speak louder than words." Still, it will not matter if no one is *listening* to those actions. We hear actions through observation, understanding, and appreciation for the act expressed. The same principles apply in our communication with God.

St. Paul tells us:

Since the creation of the world...God's eternal power and divinity have become visible, recognized through the things that he made.
—Romans 1:20

We observe an artist's creative works and we grow to know and understand the artisan. So it is with God. We observe, study, and appreciate creation and we grow in knowledge of our Creator.

We learn of God from the vast universe, grand mountains, immense oceans, renewing seasons, colorful sunsets, and natural wonders. We hear the Creator's message of life in plants that abound, animals that amaze, and the array of food that the earth produces.

Tuning in means *listening* to all the non-verbal ways God communicates with us. Creation is a loving proclamation by God. It is His answer to the human cry, "Show me."

I love to think of nature as an unlimited broadcasting station, through which God speaks to us every hour, if we only will tune in. —George Washington Carver

God can be heard through other people. The prophet Isaiah wrote: *O Lord...we are the clay and you are the potter. We are all the work of your hands* (Isaiah 64:7). Just as it is with nature, so it is with people. We grow in knowledge of the potter by observing the clay.

The Master Potter is seen in the truth, beauty, and goodness of others. The Potter is reflected in the compassion, fidelity, and forgiveness of people. Our God is known in the willing service, spirit of discovery, sense of humor, and creative works of those around us. The Potter's handiwork in and through other people challenges us to observe, comprehend, and appreciate Him.

Give ear, listen humbly,
for the Lord speaks.
—Jeremiah 13:15

God's voice speaks to us through the needs of others. He is present in the cries of the poor, the hungry, the homeless, the oppressed, the searching, the lonely, and the misunderstood. He beckons us to respond. *Love one another, as I love you* (John 15:12).

God speaks to us through the talents He has given us. Beyond the gift of life, God has equipped each of us with gifts and abilities.

He has given us talents and tools that can be used to serve others. We offer those gifts to build the Kingdom of God more fully here on earth.

We consider how our talents match the needs of those around us. That will often reveal how God wants us to act. Do we have the aptitude to teach, to heal, to feed, to build, or to entertain? Do we have a heart to parent, a love for church ministry, or knack for politics? Do we have the passion and ability to protect the environment, bring about justice, or promote peace? Or do we have the ability to awaken others to their unknown or underdeveloped talents?

God has also given us collective gifts that He uses to speak even louder and farther. There are collective gifts and abilities within our family, our nation, and our church. Together our collective gifts work to match and meet the needs of others.

God expresses himself through ourselves—to ourselves. God speaks through our conscience and common sense, our hopes and dreams, our successes and failures, our tears and laughter.

God speaks through the arts. God uses beautiful music to express his message. God uses visual arts to inspire and move our souls. God uses literature to lift us out of ourselves and teach lessons we need to hear.

Watch the Spirit

Archbishop Thomas Kelly, O.P. addressed a group of priests and told them his idea of contemplation. He said it is, "watching the Spirit at work among the people."

It takes time and effort to watch the Spirit at work in our family, in our parish, and in our world. But little by little—we will perceive and see the Spirit guide, challenge, and influence lives.

To watch the Spirit at work among us leads us to a deeper reverence for God. We also grow in appreciation, esteem, and respect for God's sanctifying power at work in our world.

Obstacles that Mute God

Obstacles can get in our way and hinder us from fully listening to God. *What are they?*

The outer noise of the world all around us are obstacles. Our lives are filled with sounds that annoy and distract.

We hear traffic, sirens, leaf blowers, and lawn mowers. We intercept the blare of TV's, CD's, PC's, iPods, cell phones, and all sorts of portable devices. The interruptions happen with the electronic squawks, alarms, and ring tones. The invasions occur with the loud, discourteous cell phone conversations.

We can't seem to escape from the *muzak* in stores, restaurants, elevators, doctor's offices, and when "on hold." We are bombarded everywhere by audio and visual advertisement. We are told over and over to spend, spend, and spend. It seems that there is a conspiracy to distract us and keep us from silence.

To listen to the voice of God takes discipline. We need quiet times away from outer noise. We need quite places free of interruptions. We need to make space so we can focus on life's really important values.

Inner noise, the obstacles of the heart, are more serious hindrances to God voice. Unforgiveness is an inner noise. Prejudice is a cacophony and clamor. Unjust anger is a disturbing clatter. Gossip is a grind and groan. Lies are a bothersome racket. Unkept promises are pandemonium. And our own critical tongue is a thunderous uproar.

In the readings, explained by the homily, God speaks to his people...and nourishes their spirit. Christ is present among the faithful through his word. —General Instruction on the Roman Missal

The Blessings of a Listening Heart

Our ability to listen to God each day begins with full participation in the Liturgy of the Word on Sunday. The ears, eyes, mind, and emotions that open on Sunday enable us to hear God speak all week.

Insights from the study of Scripture make us more aware of creation's wonders. Sensitivity to God's voice opens our hearts to the needs of others. We grow in awareness of the talents we've been given. We see the obstacles that block our hearts and hearing. We seek to be rid of those hindrances. And we find a reverent awe that comes from "just a closer walk" with Christ, all day, every day. A listening heart is the fourth step to a joyful life.

My sheep hear my voice. —John 10:27

Personal Reflection:

CHAPTER 5

A Seeking Heart

Ask and it will be given to you. Seek and you shall find. Knock and the door will be opened to you. —Matthew 6:7

Asking—A Way of Life

ℬabies depend on parents for all their needs. And infants cry to express those needs. In time and with speech, we all learned how to ask our parents and others for the things we needed. We asked parents for food, clothes, toys, etc. We asked teachers to give us knowledge. We asked friends to join us in play.

We continue to ask in our adult lives. We ask an employer for a job. We ask a doctor for health care. We ask our beloved for marriage. Our lifetime is filled with countless requests we make of others. We ask because we are in need. We ask because we want something desirable or beneficial. We ask because we are incomplete.

As people of faith, we come before our God and ask, seek, and knock. We call it the prayer of "petition." We are dependent upon God for all good things and Sunday Mass is the perfect time to place our petitions before the Lord. So, for what do we ask when we gather together?

"We" Pray for Others

The temptation is to present God with a long list of our personal needs. However, the Mass is a community prayer—a "we" prayer. Others come first. During the *Prayer of the Faithful* we pray for church leaders, civil authorities, world needs, the sick, and the deceased. We then add our own particular intentions.

During the *Eucharistic Prayer*, we again offer intercessory prayers. We pray for the pope, our bishop and clergy, all the faithful present, all the faithful departed, "and for those whose faith is known to you alone." In other words, our hearts reach out to everyone throughout the Mass.

Thy Kingdom Come

Before we receive communion, we sing or recite *The Lord's Prayer.* We pray "Thy kingdom come. Thy will be done…." It's a reminder of what Jesus taught, *Seek first the kingdom of God and His righteousness, and all these things will be given you besides* (Matthew 6:33). Personal needs aren't mentioned. Our heavenly Father knows our needs better than we do.

The prayers of petition at Mass expand our vision beyond ourselves. They open our eyes to see the needs of the people of the world. We pray for the hungry and homeless, the sick and dying, the victims of war and terror. We pray for those who face injustice, cruelty, loss, and sorrow.

Through prayer we touch the orphans, widows, refugees, and prisoners. Through prayer we touch political problems, economic difficulties, social injustice, and environmental issues. Our love for all finds its voice in our prayers of petition. These prayers we place upon the altar.

Our Father....

I cannot pray the Lord's Prayer
 and even once say "I."

I cannot pray the Lord's Prayer
 and even once say "my."

Nor can I pray the Lord's Prayer
 and not pray for another,

And when I ask for daily bread,
 I must include my brother.

For others are included in each
 and every plea,

From beginning to the end of it,
 it does not once say "me."

With Permission from *Prayers for the 12 Steps*
 —*A Spiritual Journey,* RPI Publishing, Inc.

Empowered Prayer

There is profound power in our prayers at Mass. Why? Jesus Himself is the principal celebrant. The Mass is the unbloody yet present sacrifice of Calvary in our midst. In this power, we give the contents of our hearts to Jesus to give to the Father. We make our prayers through Christ, with Christ, and in Christ—in union with the Holy Spirit. Then we can be at peace. Our lives and the life of the world are completely in God's hands.

We all have times when our minds go blank and we have no words to say. It is then I suggest that we lift our open hands—as if begging, asking, and expecting to receive. Then in faith, lift our hands up high as a sign of thanks—an offering of praise.

The Heart of Petition

Our prayers of petition are an expression of **humility**. By asking we acknowledge that without God we *can do nothing* (John 15:5).

Our prayers of petition are also an expression of **trust.** We place our lives into the hands of God. And we pray with Jesus, *Not what I will but what you will* (Mark 14:26).

Our prayers of petition are finally an expression of **faith**. We believe that *with God, all things are possible* (Matthew 19:26).

Our Pathway to Joy

At the Last Supper, the first Mass, Jesus told his apostles, *Until now you have not asked anything in my name. Ask and you will receive, so that your joy may be complete* (John 16:25). Prayer is the path. Joy is the destination.

Personal Reflection:

The Liturgy of the Eucharist
Part I — The Eucharistic Prayer

The **Liturgy of the Eucharist**, Part I, includes:

- Preparation of the Gifts, and collection,
- Prayer over the Offerings,
- Eucharistic Prayer. If we listen carefully, we will hear:
    - Thanksgiving, (especially in the Preface)
    - Acclamation, ("Holy, Holy, Holy...")
    - Invocation of the Holy Spirit
    - Institution Narrative and Consecration
    - Remembering
    - Offering
    - Intercessions
    - Final Doxology, confirmed by everyone singing the great "Amen!"

CHAPTER 6

A Grateful Heart

Give thanks to the Lord for he is good,
for his mercy endures forever.
—Daniel 3:89

Out of the Mouth of Babes

I was blessed to work with Father Herbert Tillman, C.P. at St. Agnes parish in Louisville, Kentucky. I was pastor and Father Herbert was my sage associate. His Lord called him home near his 92nd birthday. But until then he taught catechism to our first-graders.

One day, the first-grade teacher announced, "Father Herbert will celebrate his birthday soon. What would you like to do for him?"

The class stirred and chattered. Then a girl said, "Let's sing him a song."

"Fine," the teacher responded. "But what? What song will we sing?"

Then a boy shouted out, "Let's sing the lasagna song!"

The teacher raised an eyebrow and asked, "The lasagna song?"

"Oh, you know—like in church. We sing, 'Lasagna in the highest!'"

Joyful Thanksgiving

We know that "Kid's Say the Darndest Things." Why? It's because children hear the funniest things when adults speak. And what kids hear in adult singing is a mystery!

The boy who suggested the "lasagna song" for Father Herbert had the word wrong, but the right spirit. He knew the joyful attitude with which we sing.

"Hosanna" is a happy and hopeful word. It is an appropriate word when giving thanks, even for someone's birthday. And it is a most appropriate song at the conclusion of the Preface, which begins our Eucharistic Prayer at Sunday Mass.

The Mass is called the "Eucharist," which is from a Greek word that means thanksgiving. What's the best way to prepare our hearts for participation in the Eucharistic Prayer? We spend time alone or with family and friends, and count our blessings.

The Blessing of Life

Sam Walton, the founder of Wal-Mart, became a billionaire. Yet right now, you and I have something that Sam Walton doesn't. What? Sam Walton is dead. All the money in the world can't buy what we have for free at this moment. We have life. We each have this beautiful day that the Lord has made!

Without a thought, we are given every breath and beat of our heart. We have consciousness to ponder our existence and gift of life. And we have bodies with faculties and senses that allow us to experience this precious free gift of life!

Bless the Lord, my soul;
all my being, bless his holy name!
Bless the Lord, my soul;
do not forget all the gifts of God,

Who...fills your days with good things;
your youth is renewed like the eagle's.
—Psalm 103:1-2, 5

Countless Blessings

Throughout Scripture we are often instructed to recall and consider the blessings of the Lord. This step of obedience also helps us develop our attitudes of gratitude and humility.

So consider with me some of the countless blessings we receive freely with or without our knowledge.

Did you know your body has about 60,000 miles of blood vessels? A gift that's impossible to buy! Some have paid for several inches of veins for an operation. But no operation can replace a mile, let alone 60,000 miles of arteries and veins!

Did you know your brain contains about 100 billion neurons? And each neuron is capable of emitting 10 to 100 actions per second and is linked with up to 10,000 synaptic connections!* What did this brain cost us? Not a thing. A free gift! *Facts from The Johns Hopkins' Brain Institute.

Did you know your nose has 5 million scent receptors? You can pick-up over 10,000 different smells. Your nose sends neuro signals about a whiff of bacon or baked bread to awaken appetite, stimulate taste-buds, initiate salivation, and begin digestion! Other scents alert to danger, recall memories, stir emotions, arouse passion, pique pleasure, or produce peace of mind. The nose is quite a handy thing to have. And we received this nose with all its blessings for free!

Did you know your ears were designed to pick up sound waves from 20 to 20,000 cycles per second? The miraculous engineering of your inner ear cannot be matched by acoustic or computer science. Yet it is only the size of a pea! The only limit to the number of sounds you can recognize is the number of sound files stored in your memory!

Did you know your eyes can look into the distance and recognize over 100,000 objects at the same instant? Your eye's retina does more calculations and complex connections in a second than a super-computer can do in several hours. Your eyes can capture and isolate an image of a crowd of thousands at the precise exposure level. Your eyes then focus the image through lenses on a photo-sensitive retina with 120 million rods and cones. The photons are converted to electrical impulses carried through the optic nerve to your miraculous brain that recognizes that single isolated image to be the face of your loved one! And all that was a free gift!

Did you know that in addition to your material body, you have a soul? In the record of creation it is written: *The Lord God formed man out of the clay of the ground and blew into his nostrils the breath of life, and so man became a living being* (Genesis 2:7). Beyond all the faculties of our physical bodies, we each have a soul. We each have a mind, emotions, and a will. We can choose. And we have hearts that can love and spirits that can connect with God.

It's impossible to count all the blessings that we as human have been given. Yet it's easy to take human life for granted. That's why times of thoughtful reflection upon life's blessings are so important. The moments we take to meditate on all our abilities in mind, body, and soul can add great joy the day. Those first thoughtful moments can lead us into positive attitudes for every task ahead.

For we are his handiwork, created in Christ Jesus for the good works which God has prepared in advance, that we should live in them. —Ephesians 2:10

No Comparison

One day a girl was in an anxious rush to make some money. She had an idea and went to work. She approached her mother and gave her a piece of paper. It was the girl's "bill," a list of chores plus a monetary charge for each one. It read:

- For taking out the garbage—$0.75
- For washing the dishes—$1.50
- For helping dad wash the car—$2.00
- For watching my baby brother—$1.50
- For carrying in the groceries—$0.50
- For sweeping the driveway—$2.00

Total due: $8.25

The girl's mother took the bill, looked at it, and reflected for a moment. Then she sat down, turned it over, and began to write.

She wrote:

- For carrying you next to my heart as you grew for nine months—**No Charge.**
- For rocking you to sleep on my lap so many, many nights—**No Charge.**
- For nursing all your bruised knees and scarped elbows—**No Charge.**
- For the times I baked your favorite cookies—**No Charge.**
- For the times I helped you with your homework—**No Charge.**
- For wiping your tears and holding you close when you were afraid—**No Charge.**
- For always telling people what a great kid you are—**No Charge.**
- For praying for you every day—**No Charge.**

Then the mother gave the piece of paper back to her daughter. The girl took her time to read. Her head was down and face intense. She studied then paused, smiled then blushed, chuckled then quieted. At last, she cleared her throat, dried her tears, and looked at her mom.

The girl found her mother's eyes. They were full and her cheeks already wet. The daughter smiled, nodded, and grabbed the pen. She returned to her bill and wrote in large letters: "Paid in full!"

God's List

With this story in mind, let's go deeper.

There have been times in our lives when we did some good deeds—maybe extra-good. And we hoped that God would give us some special favors. Perhaps we donated a lot of money to the poor. Maybe we prayed and fasted more than usual. We volunteered at church longer than others. Or we were super patient with a cranky neighbor.

The list is real whether we write it or say it. I can see the Lord take our "good deed list," look at it carefully, and then respond:

- For giving you the gift of life—**No Charge.**
- For your family and friends—**No Charge.**
- For your body and all the marvels of your senses—**No Charge.**
- For your mind and all the wonders of learning—**No Charge.**
- For an abundance of food and drink—**No Charge.**
- For fun and laughter, and the ability to make others laugh—**No Charge.**
- For life in a free country—**No Charge.**
- For help in times of trial—**No Charge.**

- For giving you the gift of faith, and the Holy Eucharist—**No Charge.**

- For forgiveness—**No Charge.**

- For loving you so much that I sent My only Son to die on the cross for you—**No Charge.**

- For loving you so much that I sent My Holy Spirit to dwell within you—**No Charge.**

- For the hope of eternal life—**No Charge.**

This is only a partial list. Still, it's a good start—a good way to stir up thoughts and feelings of gratitude.

God's List at Mass

The Mass challenges and calls us to remember and give thanks.

The three readings at Sunday Mass help us to remember and reflect upon God's blessings: 1) the wonders of creation, 2) God's presence in our history, and 3) the words and deeds of Christ. It is fitting that we respond with, "Thanks be to God," and "Praise to you, Lord Jesus Christ."

We are ready for a longer declaration of belief and praise at the Eucharistic prayer. As the Eucharistic Prayer is proclaimed by the priest, the bread and wine on the altar become the body and blood of Christ. All present are invited to adore and give thanks.

This is the Last Supper in our midst. We are gathered around the altar because Jesus told us to *Do this in memory of me* (Luke 22:19). So we remember his death and resurrection. And we reflect on the meaning of this great mystery.

David's Victory

Remember the story about David and Goliath? Goliath was a giant man, a frightful creature, and the champion of the Philistines. He challenged the Israelites to present their own champion for mortal combat. Man-to-man fight would decide the battle. Yet no one in the Israelite army was willing to fight the beast.

So who took on the monster of a man?

The little shepherd boy named David accepted the challenge. The courageous and confident David took on the giant because of a singular belief. David knew that the Lord was and would be with him.

Goliath brandished his large sword and barked his foul curses. The brute scoffed and sneered at David's sling and stones. Then silence—David waited and listened. Then he prophesied the giant's death, declared God's glory, proclaimed Israel's victory, and ran toward the giant.

David's stone was in place, his sling on the move, and his eyes on his mark. The might of both armies stood still in a stare. Their weapons were ready yet frozen. In stunned stupor they focused on the boy who would dare.

Then the sudden stop of his feet and vault of his arm. The missile flew with force and found it's mark—dead center of the giant's head. The stone struck Goliath down and sunk deep into his brain. Then David took his head.

Wow! What a feat of faith! God's people rejoiced greatly that day. And their victory was celebrated for days and remembered for generations.

Victory Over Death

Jesus is called the "Son of David." And like David, Jesus also fought a giant. He took on a monster greater than any man. Jesus our Lord faced something much bigger than any giant.

Jesus challenged the very powers of death. And for a brief moment, it looked like death had won. Jesus submitted to the battle and entered the mortal conflict. But Jesus did not face the fight for himself. Like David, He faced the enemy for His people.

The battle was the cross and the result was necessary. Our Hero died on the cross and accomplished His goal. Easter morning revealed the Victor—Jesus risen from the dead! Death no longer had any power over Him.

As St. Paul wrote:

Where, O death, is your victory? Where, O death, is your sting? The sting of death is sin, and the power of sin is the law. **But thanks be to God who gives us the victory through our Lord Jesus Christ.** —1 Corinthians 15:55-57

What joy filled hearts once it was clear that Jesus was alive, and He had conquered death. The reality of the risen life of Jesus started a victory celebration among all His followers. But the celebration only grew with the realization of what His resurrection meant for all. This celebration and joy has lasted for two thousand years. And it continues today!

Join the Celebration

The Mass is that victory celebration! We gather and rejoice each Sunday with other followers of Jesus. We joyfully exclaim in the Eucharistic Prayer: *Christ has died. Christ has risen. Christ will come again!*

We proclaim our faith in Christ's triumph. We declare our gratitude for God's infinite power and love. We rejoice: *Christ is alive and we belong to him!*

"Good-Bye" in Hope

There is always deep sadness over the death of a loved one. Yet we Christians have the courage to stand up and proclaim to death that it doesn't have the last word. Death is a defeated foe and powerless to harm us.

We are baptized into Christ—secure in Him. And we have assurance that *just as Christ was raised from the dead by the glory of the Father, we too will live in newness of life* (Romans 6:4 and whole chapter).

> *Death is not extinguishing the light. It is putting out the lamp because the full light of dawn has come.* —Tagore

We have a spirit of peaceful celebration at funerals. We wear white vestments, display festive flowers, and sing hope-filled songs. We pray:

> *Lord, for your faithful people life is changed not ended. When the body of our earthly dwelling lies in death, we gain an everlasting dwelling place in heaven.*

We believe in the good news—the "goodbye" we say at funerals is only temporary. We shall meet again.

The celebration of the Mass is a remembrance of all that Jesus said and did. It is a celebration and renewal of our hope of eternal life. As the German proverb says, "Those who live in the Lord never see each other for the last time." And so at the end of the Eucharistic Prayer, we joyfully shout in gratitude, "Amen! Amen!"

Personal Reflection:

CHAPTER 7

A Growing Heart

*Unless the grain of wheat falls to the earth
and dies, it remains just a grain of wheat.
But if it dies, it produces much fruit.*
—John 12:24

A Tale of Two Brothers

Two brothers journeyed down the road of life. One trudged tired and worn. He dragged a cart filled with luggage: suitcases, boxes, and burdens of all sorts. He was drenched in sweat and bent by the load. He wore worry and sadness in lines on his face. And sorrow weighed heavy and slowed every pace.

The other brother had no cart—no burden to drag along. His hands were free and so was he—to laugh and dance and sing. He greeted people with a smile and offered a helping hand. He walked along in childlike awe and drank in every scene. He learned of things new and old—discoveries around every turn. He grew in skill and ability from challenges that he faced. And all-in-all he walked the road with joy and peace and grace.

What luggage did the first brother drag?

The first brother carried a heavy burden of anger. "I'm upset. I've been wronged and I won't stop until I make them pay. They've got to make this right."

The second brother seemed quite content. "I carry no grudge," he said with a smile on his face. "All people have problems, just like me. I try to understand them and I pray for them."

The first brother had given himself a lot of **unforgiveness** to carry. He also had a heavy burden of blame to drag along. "It's their fault," he repeated. "I'll not forget and I'll never forgive. I'll never release this thing."

The second brother shrugged his shoulders, lifted both hands, and said, "Freely I'm forgiven, freely I've been given, and so freely I set free!" Then he added, "I know they've harmed and hurt me, too. But I just pray 'Father in heaven, who loves all, forgive them for what they do.'"

The first brother was weighed down by **worry and fear**. What do others think of me? He wondered. "What if I fail? What do people say behind my back? What if I fall apart? What about tomorrow? What if I go broke? I'm afraid I'll die alone!"

The second brother declared, "I don't fear tomorrow or my life today. I know God is with me. He promised to stay. The troubles that come cannot compare to His power, purpose, and plan."

The first brother carried the dead weight of **prejudice**. "Those people are different. They can't be trusted. They are less-than, lower, and not worthy of concern or care."

The second brother saw the beauty and dignity of all people. He viewed all people with awe and praise. "What a variety of brothers and sisters you have given me, Lord! Your rainbow of people in colors and shapes and sizes and styles are glorious to behold!"

The first brother dragged a burden of **self-doubt**. "I'm not enough. I don't belong. I can't do it. I'm a nobody. I'm a failure. I'm no good."

The second brother was confident in faith with freedom deep within. He declared, "I am a baptized and beloved child of God. Greatness has been given me. I have a lot to offer."

The first brother wore the heavy cloak of a **critical attitude**. "Well, look at those people. They are all wrong. What fools to live that way! Look at the stupid mistakes and errors. It's all wrong!"

The second brother knew freedom with his non-judgmental attitude. He said, "I can't judge anyone— it's not my job. I have to work on that beam in my own eye before I start looking for a speck in my brother's eye."

The first brother was hampered and heavy with **gossip**. "Did you hear.... I found out that.... I was shocked to hear.... I've got to warn you about the rumor...."

The second brother refused to collect gossip and was careful not to step in any. He said, "Since Eden God covers failures, indiscretions, and sins—no exposing, stripping, or shame. So, I won't either. Instead, I see beauty in everyone. I look for the good, and then I praise and point it out in the lives of others."

The first brother bore a burden of **self-pity**. "Poor me. Life is unfair. My life is too hard. Nobody sees, nobody cares."

The second brother acknowledged his blessings, "Look at all God's goodness to me. I'm so grateful.

I've received so much. Thank you, Lord!" Gratitude released a free spirit in his heart and life.

The first brother held a heavy weight of **hypocrisy.** "I have to look good. I have to keep up the image. I say what others want to hear. And I put others down as I need to look good."

The second brother says, "Honesty is the best policy. Insincerity would wear me out. What you see is what you get." And the truth set him free.

The first brother was saddled with a **selfish** load. "Hey, I'm #1. I've got to look out for myself. No one else will. It's survival of the fittest—kill or be killed. So I'm all about me!"

The second brother considered other people worthy of his concern and help. He took time to help, lift another up, and care about the welfare of those in need around him. He was open, free, and full of enthusiasm and the joy from helping others.

Transformational Reflection

This story of the two brothers helps us reflect on our participation at Mass.

The bread and wine are brought down the aisle and placed upon the altar in the *Preparation of the Gifts*. The bread and wine represent all of us gathered for Mass.

Then the Eucharistic Prayer follows. The priest places his hands over the bread and wine and asks the Holy Spirit to transform them into the Body and Blood of Christ.

At this point, we also ask the Holy Spirit to transform us—we who are represented by the bread and wine. We ask Him to make us more and more into the Body of Christ.

What does this mean? What part of us calls out to be transformed?

We ask the Holy Spirit to transform...

- our anger into understanding,
- our unforgiveness into pardon,
- our fear into courage,
- our prejudice into tolerance,
- our self-doubt into self-confidence,
- our critical attitude into patience,
- our gossiping into appreciation,
- our self-pity into gratitude,
- our hypocrisy into honesty,
- our selfishness into self-giving,
- our brokenness into communion,
- our doubt into faith,
- our greed into generosity,
- our laziness into zeal,
- our pride into humility,
- our darkness into light, and
- our sadness into joy.

This is how we participate in the paschal mystery. This is how we pass from death to life. This is how we grow in Christian maturity.

At Mass we reflect on what needs to die in us and what needs to come alive from Him. Does our commitment to our ministry, our job, or our schoolwork need a boost? Do our relationships with others—wife, children, friends, co-workers—need to grow? Do we need to renew old dreams, discover new possibilities, or find new creativity?

Prayer for Children

In the Eucharistic Prayer for Children #1, we pray, *"Jesus brings us to you (Father). Welcome us and you welcome him."*

The prophet Isaiah said, *O Lord, you are our father. We are the clay and you the potter. We are all the work of your hand* (Isaiah 64:7). The potter forms the clay into a work of art. So God molds us and forms us more and more into the image and likeness of Christ. We submit to this lifelong process—our ongoing dying and rising.

Our Living Sacrifice

In the Eucharistic Prayer # 3, we pray, *"May he (Christ) make us an everlasting gift to you...."*

As Christ gave his all on Calvary, we too offer our total selves with Christ to the Father. We say with Jesus, *Into your hands, Father, we commend our spirit* (See Luke 23:46). That means we give our hopes and dreams, our problems and fears, our needs and our wants, our gratitude and thanks, our good deeds and even our sins.

We submit our minds, our wills and our hearts. We give it all because the Father wants it all. As Christ offers himself eternally to the Father, our inner disposition of offering remains in our hearts as we journey through each day of our lives. We are with Christ *a living sacrifice of praise.*

> *It is not enough to talk about Christ. What one has to do is let Christ enter in and take over one's life, and then let others know what that feels like.* —
> Thomas Merton

The Christ-Life Feels Like....

What does it feel like to be understanding, forgiving, and courageous? What does it feel like to live in unity with brothers and sisters? What does it feel like to be confident in faith and appreciative of others? What does it feel like to be non-judging, gracious, and truthful? What does it feel like to give love without counting the cost?

It feels like Christ is living within us—loving through us and setting us free. It feels like we are handing over our body and pouring out our blood that all may be one. Along with the apostle Paul, we exclaim, ...*I live, no longer I, but Christ lives in me* (Galatians 2:20).

> *This is the secret of joy. We shall no longer strive for our own way; but commit ourselves, easily and simply, to God's way, acquiesce in his will and in so doing find our peace.* —Evelyn Underhill

Prayer for All People

The Eucharistic Prayer is a prayer for all people. The bread and wine brought to the altar represent everyone in the world. As this bread and wine become the Body and Blood of Christ, we become more like Christ.

So we ask the Holy Spirit to look upon the needs of our world. We ask the Holy Spirit to transform the whole world more and more into the likeness of Christ. We ask Him to bring about God's kingdom more fully upon this earth. We ask Him to transform war into peace, hate into love, injustice into justice, lies into truth, hunger into satisfied stomachs, sickness into health, and the culture of death into the culture of life.

Prayer for All People

In Eucharistic Prayer # 4 we pray, *"We offer you (Father) his body and blood, the acceptable sacrifice which brings salvation to the whole world."*

Our hope for the future is not based on political wisdom, economic power, and technical ability. We look to the future with confidence because through Christ *the power of God and the wisdom of God* is among us (see 1 Corinthians 1:24).

> *A grateful heart is not only the greatest virtue, but the parent of all the other virtues.* —Cicero

Transformational Thanks

Gratitude is the fertile ground where transformation can grow. As the parent virtue, the habit of thanksgiving unlocks our hearts and opens them up for God's transforming power.

And so....

> For the transformation of bread and wine into the Body and Blood of Christ,
>
> For our ongoing transformation into the likeness of Christ,
>
> For the fuller realization of God's kingdom upon this earth,
>
> We end our Eucharistic prayer by joyfully singing, *"Amen! Amen!"*

Personal Reflection:

The Liturgy of the Eucharist
Part II — The Communion Rite

The **Liturgy of the Eucharist**, Part II, includes:

- The Lord's Prayer
- Rite of Peace
- Fraction Rite, with the "Lamb of God" acclamation
- Reception of Holy Communion by the priest and congregation
- Prayer after Communion

CHAPTER 8

A Committed Heart

I have set before you life and death,
the blessing and the curse. Choose life....
—Deuteronomy 30:19

The Old Covenant

*I*n the book of Exodus we read how Moses took the blood from sacrificed young bulls and splashed it on the altar. The altar represented God. Moses then took the blood and sprinkled it on the people as the people professed, *All that the Lord has said, we will heed and do.* This act symbolized the covenant, the bond between God and the chosen people (see Exodus 24:6-8).

What happened to these people?

Over the years many were unfaithful. They followed other gods, lost sight of the vision, and behaved immorally. The people didn't understand how God was committed to them. And the people didn't have an effective way to renew their part of the covenant.

Our New Covenant

To remedy the situation God decided to do what only God could do. He did not choose to send a new sacrificial animal or even a whole flock of animals. Instead, God sent his only Son, whose body was broken and whose blood was poured out for us. In Christ, all would realize the profound commitment of God to us. The sacrifice of Jesus on the cross is the Father's proclamation of the new covenant.

For our part, we are not sprinkled with animal blood. Instead, we are given the Body of Christ to eat and the Blood of Christ to drink. This is how we renew our part of the covenant. This is how we commune, enter into union, and are intimately joined with our God.

Total Dedication

The same reality can be stated this way. Jesus didn't look down upon our troubled world and say, "I'll go to earth and try to give them a hand." Instead, Jesus said, "I'll become one with the human race. I will give my life for them."

Jesus demonstrated absolute loyalty and total dedication to us. Jesus was, and still is, God's invitation for us to be his people. Jesus' sacrifice is God's "Amen" to his part of the new covenant. Our spoken "Amen" at Communion is our acceptance.

Commitment

I find inspiration in some past statements of commitment. During World War II, Winston Churchill, the prime minister of Great Britain, declared:

> Here is the answer which I will give to President Roosevelt.... We shall not fail or falter; we shall not weaken or tire. Neither the sudden shock of battle nor the long-drawn trial of vigilance and exertion will wear us down. Give us the tools and we will finish the job.

During the Cold War of the 1960's the American President John F. Kennedy proclaimed:

> Let every nation know, whether it wishes us well or ill, that we shall pay any price, bear any burden, meet

any hardship, support any friend, oppose any foe to assure the survival and the success of liberty.

More to our point, we have these words of Robert Moorehead:

> My goal is heaven ... my mission is clear. I cannot be bought, compromised, detoured, lured away, turned back, diluted or delayed. I will not flinch in the face of sacrifice, hesitate in the presence of adversity... ponder at the pool of popularity, or meander in a maze of mediocrity. I won't give up, shut up, let up or slow up.

St. Paul reveals his determined will in his epistle to the Romans:

> *What will separate us from the love of Christ? Will anguish, or distress, or persecution, or famine, or nakedness or peril, or the sword... I am convinced that neither death, nor life, nor angels, nor principalities, nor present things, nor future things, nor powers, nor height, nor depth, nor any other creature will be able to separate us from the love of God in Christ Jesus our Lord.* —Romans 8:35, 38-39

Peter's Commitment

The Apostle Peter speaks some of Scriptures most moving words. On the night before Jesus died, Peter denied him three times. Then after the resurrection on the seashore in Galilee, Jesus tests Peter's commitment:

> *Jesus asked him, "Peter, do you love me?"*
>
> *And Peter responded, "Yes, Lord, you know that I love you."*
>
> *A second time Jesus asked Peter, "Do you love me?"*
>
> *Again, Peter replied, "Yes, Lord, you know that I love you."*
>
> *And a third time Jesus asked, "Peter, do you love me?"*

> *Peter became emphatic. "Lord, you know all things. You know that I love you.* (See John 21: 15-19).

At Communion time, we are asked to acknowledge our belief in Jesus' Eucharistic presence. And like Peter, we are also asked, "Do you love me?" Our "Amen" is our "Yes." Our "Amen" is our public pronouncement that we want to be the best of friends to Jesus.

Total Dedication

There is a transforming power behind our "Amen." This response resonates deep in our soul. In truth we declare:

> *"Yes, Lord, I choose you, entrust myself to you, covenant myself to you, dedicate myself to you and devote myself to you. I will not fail or falter. I will pay any price, bear any burden. My mission is clear. I cannot be detoured. Nothing will separate me from you. Lord, you know all things. You know that I love you. I love you totally, completely, absolutely, and forever."*

Here we touch the core of what it means to be a follower of Jesus. The depth, sincerity, and ironclad conviction of our "Amen" as we partake in Holy Communion directs the energy of our minds, hearts, and wills in every moment of our lives.

> *To say yes, you have to sweat and roll up your sleeves and plunge both hands into life up to the elbows.* —Jean Anouilh

Examples of Commitment

We look to Christ as our prime example. He reminds us, *No one has greater love than this, to lay down one's life for one's friends* (John 15:13). He proclaimed it, and then he did it. His death on the cross was his act of absolute obedience to his Father. And it was his statement of unconditional love for us.

The "yes" of Mary to become the mother of Jesus is our second example of commitment. *Behold I am the handmaid of the Lord. May it be done to me according to your word* (Luke 1:38).

Thirdly, we have the examples of martyrs throughout the centuries. Their commitment and courage reminds us of the depth of dedication that is possible when one says "Amen" to God.

At Communion time we announce, *Here I am, Lord. I come to do your will.* (See 1 Samuel 3; Hebrews 10:7-9).

Our Loyalty

For Christians, our most basic loyalty is not to a cause, a creed, or an ideal. It is to a person. When asked about the greatest commandment, Jesus responded,

You shall love the Lord your God with all your heart, with all your soul, and with all your mind. This is the greatest and first commandment.

Jesus meant a no-holds-barred total giving of self. Then he added, *The second is like it. You shall love your neighbor as yourself* (Mt 22:37-39). Our "Amen" at Communion immerses us in his love for all people.

Our loyalty, commitment, and love all began at our baptism. Through this sacrament God said to us, "I take you as my child." And we said (or our parents said for us) "I take you Lord as my God." This covenant commitment was refreshed and strengthened by the sacrament of Confirmation.

And now, we renew this bond with God each time we present ourselves at Holy Mass. The "Amen" we say as we receive Holy Communion is the confirmation of our ongoing choice of Christ. It is our expressed intention to follow through and serve the Body of Christ.

Enthusiasm

The result should be a fervent feeling of excitement. The English word "enthusiasm" is a compound of Greek words: *en* plus *theos*—meaning "in" plus "God." The same power that makes grass grow, flowers bloom, and eagles soar abides in us.

Our "Amen" has invited God to enter in and take our life to do His will. We invite God to be present in the world through us. We allow God to teach through us, heal through us, bring peace through us, and love through us. In other words, *Your kingdom come, Your will be done* through us.

Communion Unity

After the Communion Rite, imagine everyone in church standing in a large circle with hands held. This image reminds us of why Jesus gave us the Mass.

Jesus prayed aloud to His Father during the Last Supper. He prayed for his disciples that *they may all be one, and you Father are in me and I am in you* (John 17:21). Our dream is to have the whole world hold hands—to be one in peace. Our union through Holy Communion gives us hope that this dream will be realized more and more each day.

> *Out of the darkness of my life, so much frustrated, I put before you the one great thing to love on earth: the Blessed Sacrament ... There you will find romance, glory, honor, fidelity, and the true way of all your loves upon earth ... which every man's heart desires.* —J.R.R. Tolkien

Broken Bread

At the Last Supper Jesus took bread, blessed it, broke it, and gave it as food to those who needed help. That bread was and is his body. We are members of his body.

So we can say that at Mass Jesus takes us, blesses us, breaks us, and gives us as food to those who need help.

- He breaks our selfishness
    —so we become self-giving.
- He breaks our unforgiveness
    —so we become reconcilers.
- He breaks our prejudices
    —so we remove barriers between us.
- He breaks our fears
    —so that we are free to love.

It is all part of that lifelong process of dying to self that others may live. His broken bread is meant to be shared—it has the power to bring wholeness to our world.

How will the world around us know that we have celebrated Mass on Sunday?

In the Acts of the Apostles, we read:

When the people saw the boldness of Peter and John, and perceived that they were uneducated, common men, they wondered; and they recognized that they had been with Jesus. —Acts 4:13

All week people will see our dedication to truth, enthusiasm for justice, compassion for the poor, spirit of forgiveness, unity in community, and boldness to live our faith. They will recognize that we, too, have been with Jesus. His joy within us will touch those around us.

I have come that you may have life and have it to the full. —John 10:10

Personal Reflection:

The Rite of Sending Forth

The **Concluding Rites** include:

- A Greeting
- Last Blessing
- The Charge to...

"Go in peace to love and serve the Lord."

CHAPTER 9

A Serving Heart

Christ has no body now on earth, but yours, no hands but yours, no feet but yours. Yours are the eyes from which the compassion of Christ will look out upon the world. Yours are the feet with which Christ is to go about doing good and yours are the hands with which Christ is to bless us now. —St. Teresa of Avila

The Mass Continues...

"The Mass is ended. Go in peace." We used to think that these words ended our participation in Holy Mass. But as a matter of fact those words are just the beginning.

Where does the Mass take place?

The Mass takes place in church, at home, at work, in school, on the street, at the store, etc. But first, it takes place within our hearts, minds, and attitudes.

When does the Mass take place?

The Mass takes place at the appointed hour on Sunday morning. But it doesn't stop—it continues for the next seven days. The Mass in church on Sunday expresses our community life. It is our limited time together to celebrate and encourage one another in our common faith, hope, and life. All so we can continue the celebration of faith throughout the week.

A People for Others

At the end of the Eucharistic Prayer we sing "Amen." We join ourselves with Christ's sacrifice on Calvary. We identify ourselves as his church—a people like Him, given for others.

Christ offered his body and blood that all may be one. We offer ourselves as living sacrifices to God. We offer ourselves so that the Kingdom of God may be realized in and through us.

We used to say that we live in the world, and go to church on Sunday. Now we realize that **we are the church**—sent out to the world on Sunday. We have a mission. We have a purpose. It is through our compassion and our service that our actions at Mass are expressed and verified.

Come, See, Go, Tell

There are two words the Lord used frequently in the Gospels. The first word is "come."

Come, follow me....
Come and see....
Come, take up your cross....
Come after me, and I will make you....
Come to me, all you who labor and are burdened....

The second word that Jesus used is "go."

Go in peace....
Go and show yourselves to the priest....
Go and tell John what you have seen and heard....
Go tell my brethren they are to go to Galilee....
Go into the whole world and preach the gospel....

Why *come* to Christ, but *go* nowhere with the gifts he gives? Why *go* out to do something—but not first *come* to Christ to be taught and nourished?

On Sunday we *come* to Christ to listen, give thanks, be fed, and support one another. And then we *go* out into the world to serve Christ in our neighborhoods.

We *come* in need—we *go* forth empowered. The weekly rhythm of the Mass: *come* to Mass and *go* forth to live sets the course of our week. And it gives meaning to the statement that the Mass is the "source and the summit" of our spiritual lives, lives that are centered on Christ.

Sent Out

We might compare participation in Sunday Mass to the time the disciples spent with Jesus after their mission trip. Jesus had sent them out two-by-two and they returned with joy to reconnect and receive more (see Luke 10:17-24). Their Kingdom ministry was filled with excitement, wonders, mistakes, miracles, strange-events, good-news, insights, and mysteries. They had much to relate to the Lord and lots of questions.

At Mass on Sunday morning we reconnect and share with the Lord and other disciples after our week. We celebrate successes, report miracles, share experiences, and relate our discoveries. We also share our struggles, ask for help, express our needs, find healing for failures, gain new insight, learn more about the Kingdom, and receive strength for the challenges ahead.

Sent Out to....

The **Rite of Dismissal** is our sending forth. What is it that we are being sent out to do?

In general terms and answer:

- We are sent out to live the gospel.
- We are sent out to do works of justice.
- We are sent out to witness to God's love.

The practical applications of those spiritual principles are activities and service that build God's Kingdom. This may include time spent to teach catechism, serve at a soup kitchen, work on pro-life activities, or care for an elderly parent or neighbor. It may mean that we will blow the whistle on an unjust, illegal, or harmful business activity. It may mean that we will be politically active or volunteer to serve on a church project.

Our service for the Kingdom also embraces our service, ministry, and sacrificial-love toward our spouse, children, family, and friends. It includes our efforts for school, work, community and other responsibilities.

Our service for the Kingdom means that we are people of integrity. We speak the truth, show compassion, extend hospitality, and offer a good example for others.

Service is about more than doing something—*it's about being somebody*. The heart of ministry is relationship. Our personhood is at the heart of our service.

Bread Given

What happens to us when we receive the Holy Eucharist—the Bread of Life?

St. Augustine tells us, "You are what you have received." Pope Leo I said, "We are transformed into what we have consumed." That means we become, like Christ, bread for others. That is our identity.

It doesn't take much searching to find where we can put that identity to work.

- The lonely and afraid need the bread of companionship.
- The worried need the bread of encouragement.
- The ignorant and doubtful need the bread of truth.
- The estranged need the bread of forgiveness.
- The oppressed need the bread of justice.

- The bereaved and those in tears need the bread of compassion.
- Our world longs for the bread of peace.

To whom much is given, much will be expected. — Luke 12:48

A man walked and talked to God in prayer. He'd seen a lot of hardship and hurt in the world and all along his journey. In a fit, he pointed to the pain and problems— all the suffering in the world. The man asked God, "When are you going to do something about all this?"

God responded, "I did. I created you."

"I Could Have Won...."

One day a rich boy and a poor boy got into a fight. The rich boy won the scuffle, though his opponent was bigger. The poor boy wiped a bloody lip, looked up, and said, "I could have won. If I could have a bowl of soup twice a week like you do, I'd be as strong as you are!"

The other boy's words made a deep impression on the rich boy. He refused the soup at dinner that night and would not wear his fine coat. He wore mittens instead of gloves and clogs instead of boots. He shunned his privilege and experienced the poverty of his classmates and friends.

That single schoolyard event changed the course of his entire life. The boy dedicated himself to a life of service with special concern for the poor and needy. Much had been given to him, and he knew much would be expected of him. He became a missionary, a doctor, a philosopher, and a philanthropist. In 1952, Dr. Albert Schweitzer received the Nobel Peace Prize.

Get Ready

Commit to God and truly desire to do His will—then get ready. God may present you with a major calling. He may speak to your heart and say, "I want you to join the Peace Corps." Or "I want you to teach in the inner city." "I want you to run for public office." Or "I want you to be a priest."

You and I may gulp and say, "Who, me? I can't do that, Lord. I am unable. I am unworthy. I am not strong enough." But the Lord doesn't pay any attention to our fears.

God asked Moses to lead his people out of slavery in Egypt and into freedom in the Promised Land. Moses felt inadequate. He claimed to be a poor speaker. Moses told God, *Who am I that I should go to Pharaoh and lead the Israelites out of Egypt?*

The Lord answered, *I will be with you* (Exodus 3:11-12).

God asked Jeremiah to be his prophet and proclaim his message to the people. Jeremiah protested, *Ah, Lord God, I know not how to speak. I am too young.*

The Lord answered, *I am with you* (see Jeremiah 1:6,7).

God asked Gideon to save his people from the power of Midian. Gideon replied, *Please, Lord, how can I save Israel? My family is the lowest in Manasseh, and I am the most insignificant in my father's house.*

The Lord answered him, *I shall be with you* (Judges 6:15-16).

Willing yet Weak

The apostles abandoned Jesus in his final hours of need. Even Peter was afraid and denied him. They must have felt like total losers. They must have faced their failures in the presence of the resurrected Christ. They had let him down.

But Jesus said to them, *As the Father sent me, so I send you* (John 20:21).

They probably thought, "Who, us? You've got to be kidding. We are the ones who deserted you. We are weak, inadequate failures."

And what did Jesus tell them? *I am with you always* (Matthew 28:20).

Jesus was telling them, and us, that if you depend on your wisdom, your strength and your power, you will be helpless. But if you realize your limitations and open yourself up to receive the Spirit I will give you, then you will be fearless, eloquent, powerful, successful, and faithful even unto death.

And that's what happened. All but John died as martyrs.

> *A ship is safe in harbor,*
> *but that's not what ships are for.*
> —William Shedd

Serve One Another

Visual images can instruct, inspire, and imprint messages that endure in our hearts and minds. That's why I would like to see a pitcher of water, a basin, and a towel (or a visual image of them) at the church exits. It would remind everyone that they are to "wash one another's feet"—to serve one another.

Jesus served his disciples in that way at the Last Supper. He washed their feet. Jesus on his knees as a servant was the image left in the hearts and minds of his disciples.

But foot-washing may be too remote for us today. Few of us are likely to wash feet this week. These images might not move us.

Perhaps a better symbol at the doors might be an ear and a tongue. A picture of these on a banner would serve as a practical reminder. Every day, every week, all year long we have unlimited opportunities to serve others with our ears and tongue. We serve with ears that listen well in love. We serve with words spoken to benefit, edify, encourage, and offer hope to another in love.

The Art of Listening

The sensitive art of listening requires great sacrifice. There are few who gain mastery. Most are unwilling to face the profound death to self that listening requires. But those who learn to listen will also find the words to bless.

The ministry to speak the right word follows the listening ear. First we hear, understand, perceive, and become attuned to another person. Then we hear beyond the words. We sense the feelings and needs of another.

Then our words of encouragement, words of praise, words of wisdom, words of affection, words of appreciation, and even words of admonition will be heard. Our words will be welcome, accepted, and appreciated—just what they needed to hear.

The greatest good you can do for another is not just to share your riches, but to reveal to him his own. —
Benjamin Disraeli

It is in the sensitive use of our ears and our tongue that we do the greatest good. We reveal to others the riches they already possess. What joy we will have in our hearts and what joy we will bring into this world when we serve others with our ears and tongue.

Personal Reflection:

CHAPTER 10

A Compassionate Heart

Put on then, as God's chosen ones,
holy and beloved, heartfelt compassion....
—Colossians 3:12

Quotes on Compassion

*H*ere are more quotes from my collections. These are on the subject of compassion.

> *A tear dries quickly, especially when it is shed for the trouble of others.* —Cicero

> *The comforter's head never aches.* —Italian Proverb

> *We must learn to regard people less in the light of what they do or omit to do, and more in the light of what they suffer.* —Dietrich Bonhoeffer

> *Compassion is the basis for all morality.* —Arthur Schopenhauer

A Mile in Moccasins

I read a story some years ago about a young boy who wanted a dog.

He and his dad went to a home where there were five dogs for sale, four healthy ones and a one with a bad leg. The boy, who was crippled, chose the dog with the bad leg. He knew they would understand each other.

To understand and to be understood are two of life's greatest challenges. They are also two of life's greatest rewards—exhilarating and rare.

The old Indian adage reminds us, "You don't really know another until you have walked a mile in his moccasins." Actually, a mile is just the beginning. To truly understand another takes a lifetime—a lifetime of asking, listening, observing, being sensitive, paying attention, and growing aware.

I wonder what would happen if the leaders of warring nations spend a few days living on the enemy's side?

The leaders would find a lot of ordinary people. They'd find people who work hard to make a living and raise a family. They'd find people with illness and emotional problems. They'd find people who want to speak, worship, and associate freely. They'd find people who desire happiness, peace, safety, security, and an end to all the violence.

A leader who walked with people on the other side would learn and feel things. A leader who broke bread with people on the other side would grow in understanding. A leader who saw these others laugh, cry, suffer, and rejoice would be motivated to change things. That leader would return to make life better and happier for all sides.

> *The rain said to the wind,*
> *"You push and I'll pelt."*
> *They so smote the garden bed*
> *That the flowers actually knelt,*
> *And lay lodged— though not dead.*
> *I know how the flowers felt.*
> —Robert Frost

The Heart of Jesus

How often in the gospels we read these words?

Jesus had compassion on the multitude.
—Matthew 9:36

When the Lord saw her,
he was moved with pity for her....
—Luke 7:13

My heart is moved with pity for the crowd.
—Mark 8:2

Before he acted, Jesus felt. He felt sorrow for the hardship people faced. He felt grief for the losses people suffered. He felt concern for the needs people had. And he felt moved by the lack of a shepherd among the sheep.

Sometimes the best way for us to prepare for worship on Sunday is to read the newspaper. It is here that we see our human family. We get a glimpse of what so many suffer, face, and feel. We read about the victims of war, terrorism, fires and floods. We read about those who suffer from hunger, homelessness, unemployment and poverty. We read about the long list of human problems suffered by real people.

From personal experience, empathy, or imagination we say, as Jesus would, "I feel and acknowledge the plight of the people in that place." That understanding moves us to pray for others. And that compassionate connection with our Lord motivates and empowers us to go forth and serve.

Carry the Cross—Comfort Christ

Had we lived in the time of Jesus' passion, we would have wanted to help him—especially along the way of the cross.

Perhaps, like Veronica, we could have wiped his brow. Like Simon of Cyrene, we could have carried the wood of the cross. Like his mother, Mary, we could have encouraged him with looks of love. Like his friends in the crowd, we could have shouted words of thanks and praise. Or like the apostle John, we could have stood by the cross and assured him of our friendship.

In truth, we can do all that and more.

How is that possible?

It is possible because the Passion of Christ continues in our midst, today.

Jesus Is Among Us

The Acts of the Apostles records that Saul of Tarsus persecuted early Christians. Then while on the road to Damascus, a light from the sky flashed around him. He fell to the ground and heard a voice ask him, *Saul, Saul, why are you persecuting me?*

Saul asked, *Who are you, sir?*

The reply came, *I am Jesus whom you are persecuting* (See Acts 9:4-5).

How could Saul be persecuting Jesus? Jesus had suffered and died on the cross long before this event.

Saul soon came to realize that Jesus identified with the pain and suffering of the young Christian community. Indeed, Jesus identifies himself with the pain and suffering of the whole human family.

His Passion Continues

Consider with me some examples of the Lord's Passion today. ***The Stations of the Cross*** help us structure and sense the suffering of Jesus. With hearts and minds open, we can visualize the people and places where Jesus is now. In identification, his passion continues.

Jesus Agonizes in the Garden

This scene brings to mind all who suffer anxiety and worry through depression, self-doubt, and fear. Think of those who agonize over finances, health issues, and difficult decisions. Or think of those who suffer regrets, heartache, and loneliness.

Jesus is Scourged at the Pillar

We consider now all the people who endure the scourge of war, the pangs of hunger, the sting of poverty, and the strips of homelessness. Consider those punished in political oppression, injustice, and cruelty. Consider the victims of torture. Consider spouses, children, or seniors who are abused by family. Consider the scourge on our environment, the abuse upon the gift of this earth: ***the Passion of the Planet.***

Jesus is crowned with Thorns

Under this station we imagine all those mocked, insulted, and disrespected. Imagine the victims of prejudice, injustice, and racial intolerance. Imagine those rejected, misunderstood, or not appreciated. And again remember creation which groans under the curse and crown of thorns from the fall of man. (See Genesis 3:18 and Romans 8:819-22).

Jesus is Condemned

Here we remember all those victims of lies, especially the falsely accused, betrayed, and unjustly imprisoned. Remember those condemned by illiteracy, the lack of education, lost opportunities, and poverty. Remember those condemned by poor health caused by the lack of clean water, sanitation, and medicine.

Jesus Falls under the Cross

Now we might reflect on those weighed down by physical illness, chronic disabilities, or emotional distress. Reflect on those who fail at school, work, career, or relationships. Reflect on those laden with memories of long lost hopes, dreams, visions, and goals taken by life's hardship. Reflect on those burdened by the limitations of old age. And reflect on those who fall under selfishness and sin.

Jesus is Stripped of his Garments
This station brings to mind all those stripped of their rights. We think of those stripped of the right to vote, the right to free speech, and the rights of basic human dignity that we take for granted here. We think of those stripped of their ability to remember or think clearly due to Alzheimer's, Parkinson's, strokes, mental disorders, or other mental disabilities. We think of victims of natural disasters stripped of land, home, possessions, or loved ones. And in times of economic hardships we think of those stripped of jobs, savings, dignity, hope, opportunities, home, security, and life as they had known it.

Jesus is Nailed to the Cross
Here we include and imagine those people who are limited by physical challenges. We imagine those limited by addictions to drugs, alcohol, substances, or harmful behaviors. We imagine those limited by injustice—without freedom to assemble, worship, associate, or pursue the life they desire. And we imagine those limited by crippling fear—whatever the source.

Jesus Dies on the Cross
Under this station we remember all the victims of abortion. We remember those killed in wars, the ones who served, ones forced to fight, innocents caught in crossfire, and the death of peace. We remember the victims of terror, the innocents who die, and the heroes who gave all. We remember the victims of genocide, ethnic cleansing, and racial holocaust. We remember the victims of gang violence, drive by shootings, and the collateral killings in our city streets. We remember those killed by drunk drivers and drivers distracted

by cell phones. We remember those who suffered divorce and the death of a relationship or friendship. We remember those who faced the death of hope, a dream, or a vision. And we remember the part of us that dies within us even as we live.

If you want to make another happy, show compassion. If you want to be happy, show compassion. —Dali Lama

Help that Continues

Along the way of the cross, there were people who hurt Jesus. But there were also people who helped and consoled our Lord. That helping continues today.

Jesus Meets His Mother

Here we think of parental love and family support. We think of those people who encourage others and cheer them on in the midst of life's hardships and struggles. We think of those who are patient and understanding.

Veronica Wipes Jesus' Face

This station brings to mind those who show tenderness. We consider all those who offer comfort and console. We consider those who comfort even in difficult and dangerous situations—who console even in the presence of profound suffering.

Simon Helps Jesus Carry the Cross

Here we recognize all those in helping professions. We recognize those who serve as police and fire-fighters, teachers and coaches, doctors and nurses, care-givers and hospice workers, priests and nuns, lawyers and judges, scientists and entertainers, counselors and environmentalists, etc.

Mary Receives the Dead Body of Jesus & Buries Him

With Mary we find all those people who assist the bereaved.

The Resurrection of Jesus

Wherever we help people, we find life and joy, health and happiness, forgiveness and reconciliation, hope and enthusiasm, unity and friendship. We help others, and we know that the risen Lord Jesus is alive and well within us. This is what we celebrate when we profess, **"Christ has died. Christ is risen. Christ will come again."**

Opportunities in the Mass

At Sunday Mass we are given a number of gifts and opportunities. We have the opportunity to see beyond our limited life and envision the world. We are given the opportunity for big dreams. We dream of a kingdom where justice and peace reign, where all human life is reverenced and respected, where basic human needs are met, where the planet is protected, and where the Creator is honored and adored.

These dreams are ours for the taking. But their reality and the true experience come as we say, **"Into your hands, Father, we commend our spirit."** Then the compassion of Christ will flow through us and move us to act.

> *We are called to play the Good Samaritan on life's roadside; but that will be only an initial act. One day the whole Jericho road must be transformed so that men and women will not be beaten and robbed as they make their journey through life. True compassion is more than flinging a coin to a beggar; it understands that an edifice that produces beggars needs restructuring.* —J.R.R. Tolkien

Remembering Jesus

When Jesus gave us the Mass, he said, *Do this in memory of me* (Luke 2:19). He didn't mean to recall history. Jesus asked us to remember the mystery of his eternal offering of himself to his Father. And also to remember his Father's loving acceptance of him.

With boundless compassion and love, Jesus looks upon us, embraces us, and takes us with himself to the Father. And the Father accepts us as members of the Body of Christ.

The human family shares in the dying and rising of Jesus. It is to experience loving and being loved. Through the cross of Jesus, we are reconciled with the Father. We rejoice in the knowledge that our heavenly Father is "merciful and gracious, slow to anger, most loving and true" (Psalm 86:15).

As a father has compassion on his children,
so the Lord has compassion on the faithful.
—Psalm 103:13

Let It Shine

The old cathedral was a site to behold with its ancient art, ornate woodwork, and stained glass masterpieces. The tour guide offered spiritual and cultural insights that satisfied most of the tourists. But one little girl was curious about the people depicted in the windows.

"Who are those people?" The girl asked and pointed to a large and colorful stained glass window.

"Saints," the tour guide answered.

"Oh!" The sun was bright, the window large, and the girl was tiny in comparison. The sight overwhelmed her.

The tour guide began to move, but the girl was still awestruck and curious. "Hey, wait," she called out. "What do saints do?"

The tour guide didn't want to spend time on a lesson about the saints. So he just said, "Saints do good things for God."

That evening before bedtime prayers, the little girl had an announcement for her mother. "I know what saints do, Mommy. I know the good thing they do for God."

"Really. What is it?" Her mother asked.

"Saints let the light shine right through them!"

Participation at Mass transforms our minds and our hearts. We who are open and willing participants become like those in the stained glass windows. We allow God's light, love, truth, and compassion to shine through us. Then others are inspired and warmed by the good things that come from our Father above.

> *All good giving and every perfect gift is from above, coming down from the Father of lights, with whom there is no alteration or shadow caused by change.*
> —James 1:17

Personal Reflection:

CHAPTER 11

A Joyful Heart

I have told you this so that my joy may be in you and your joy may be complete. —*John 15:11*

*H*as this ever happened to you? You are watching a basketball game on TV. The score is tied. Your team has the ball. There are ten seconds left to play. You are on the edge of your seat and…there is a break for a commercial! #@%!&!

It is not only upsetting that commercials come at the most inconvenient time. It's also upsetting because what they often communicate to us is a lie. I don't mean that they are lying to us about a specific product. This may happen. It's the **big lie** I'm talking about. Commercials tell us over and over again that, "To be happy, you've got to have stuff." "To be happy you've got to have beer, cars, perfume, clothes, soap, medicine...."

It is estimated that by the time a child enters first grade, he or she has seen over 30,000 commercials. Thirty thousand times they have heard the message that, "To be happy, you've got to have stuff."

After hearing the message so many times, some people are actually dumb enough to believe it. So they go off and buy lots of stuff. This stuff doesn't seem to make them happy, so they work harder, earn more money, and go off and buy more stuff. Still no happiness. So they work even harder, earn even more money, and buy even more stuff. Still no happiness. Guess what? It's not working. So they get frustrated and depressed. Could it be they are looking for joy in all the wrong places?

Once upon a time there was a king who was very anxious and depressed. He longed to be really happy but didn't know what to do. He called in his sage to give him some advice. The sage said, "There is but one cure for you, O King. You must sleep one night in the shirt of a happy man."

The king dispersed his servants throughout the kingdom to search for a man who was truly happy. Most everyone they found had some cause for misery, something that robbed them of true and complete happiness. Then one day they found a man, sitting on the side of a road, sporting a broad and genuine smile. He was a beggar. When the servants asked him if he was happy, he smiled. "As a matter of fact, I am very happy," the man replied. Then they told him of their mission. The king wanted to be happy and he was advised to sleep one night in the shirt of a truly happy man. Would the beggar sell them his shirt so that they could take it back to the king? The man smiled and then burst out into laughter. "I am sorry, but I cannot oblige the king. I haven't a shirt on my back."

The king had a lot to think about that night.

Jesus tells us of the man who found a pearl of great price and sells all he has and buys it (Matthew 13:46). The ultimate pearl of great price is not a pearl at all, nor a diamond, nor a stack of million dollar bills. The pearl is Jesus. Where do you find him? The central theme of this book is that Jesus is found at Mass, in Word, in Sacrament, and in the gathered Community. And Jesus is found throughout the week when what we do at Mass in put into action. Full, conscious and active participation at Mass means full, conscious, and active participation in life.

The Source

Christ is always present in his Church, especially in her liturgical celebrations.
—Constitution on the Sacred Liturgy, Ch. 1, #7

To say that the Mass is the "source and summit" of our Catholic faith is another way to say that Jesus is the center of our lives. Jesus is the summit toward which the activity of the church is directed (cf. opus cited, #10). He is also the fount that overflows with joy. The spiritual concepts, habits, attitudes, and actions set forth in this book lead to joyful living. How? It is because these things lead us into a closer intimacy with the Lord Jesus. It is he who makes us a joyful people. It is he who fills us with a joy that surpasses all understanding.

The Eucharist must become the center of our lives. Anyone who has really discovered Christ must lead others to Him. This is a joy we must not keep to ourselves. It must be passed on. —Benedict XVI

If we go through life with a
  humble heart,
      forgiving heart,
        welcoming,
            listening heart,
              asking heart,
                grateful heart,
                  transforming heart,
                    committed heart,
                      serving heart, and a
                        compassionate heart,
                          we end up with a joyful heart.

On days when we are feeling down and out, I suggest we simply go down this list and reflect on how well we are putting into practice these ten attitudes expressed at Mass. For instance, if we measure ourselves on a scale of one to ten, we might decide we are a "7" on hospitality. Then we need to ask, "What would it take to make that a "10"? Do this for each of the steps. If we are brave, we might even ask our spouse, a brother or sister, a good friend, a teacher or coach how they think we could reach "10." We are a work in progress. Sunday Mass challenges us to keep growing, step by step, individually and as a community.

Celebrate!

The strength to see the good side of things should be characteristic of a Christian. If the Gospel really means "good news," then being a Christian means being a happy person, one who spreads joy. "Gloomy faces," said St. Philip, "aren't made for the happy house of Paradise." —Pope John Paul I

All that is left now is to celebrate! Join hands, jump up, sing out loud, and dance with joy. Do some cartwheels, somersaults, head stands, and celebrate. God's love is in our midst!

You gladden us with the joy of your presence.
—Psalm 21:7

Personal Reflection:

All Week Long

Sharpen the Axe

$\mathcal{A}$braham Lincoln once observed: "If I had eight hours to chop down a tree, I'd spend the first six sharpening my axe." The time and effort spent on preparation makes any task much easier.

The same is true in professional and collegiate sports. A team will put in a whole week of practice for a one hour game! According to Joe Paterno, longtime football coach for Penn State, "The will to win is important, but the will to prepare is vital.

From my early chapters till now, I have stressed the value I place on preparation. I have stated that the Mass is a celebration, a feast, and a renewal of spiritual life. It is a life changing experience. It is intended to empower us for the week ahead, in service and continued connection to God and others. But many people say they don't get all these things from the Mass. They don't experience the celebration and joy I talk about.

Why not?

In the Introduction, I noted that it was inaccurate to call the presiding priest "the celebrant." It not proper because everyone present for worship is a celebrant. I shared my hope that everyone would actively participate in the Mass. But I made it clear that whole-hearted-active participation requires preparation of heart, mind, soul, and attitude in the week before.

Sharpen the Soul

Our preparation and attitude adjustments prior to the Mass are far more important than cutting down a tree.

We do far more that sharpen an axe. We prepare and sharpen our souls. We prepare for important Kingdom work, intimate connection with the Lord Jesus Christ, and fellowship with other members of Christ's Church—his Body.

From *The Humble Heart* chapter on, I showed the many ways we prepare ourselves in advance for the Mass. I suggested attitude adjustments, character corrections, prayerful practices, practical actions, and more. I shared steps to help anyone prepare for full and joyful participate in the celebration on Sunday morning.

I believe, practice, and teach these things. I seek to prepare my heart, mind, spirit, and attitude. I remember the story of the moment Mary, with Jesus in her womb, entered the home of Elizabeth, her cousin. John the Baptist yet within Elizabeth's womb leaped for joy! Then Elizabeth was filled with the Holy Spirit and she prophesied and there was great joy in celebration of the Lord Jesus—present within Mary!

So I prepare for and go to the Mass with that same joyful anticipation. Jesus will be there. He is in present in the holy Mass. And Jesus is present in his people, the living tabernacles of the Body of Christ.

I am never disappointed, unless I fail to prepare. I learned that for me to get something out of the Mass each Sunday, I need to put something in.

What is that something?

Preparation!

Attitudes of the Heart

All the attitudes of "The Heart" that I have shared are *the ten habits of the joyful life!*

The quantity and quality of our joy depends on how we practice these habits. It's not enough to read this material. It is important to understand and practice these spiritual habits, attitudes, and actions.

Here's what I suggest. Go back through the book, review each chapter, note what you've highlighted, and meditate on the concepts. Then in the space provided at chapter's end: 1) journal a summary of your thoughts, 2) list practical ways to live the lessons, and 3) note other insights or actions that surfaced.

To Do . . . .

Along with the insights and actions that you noted, I would like to offer the following suggestions:

1) Humility

❏ Read the book of Job chapters 38 to 42.
❏ Read Psalm 127.
❏ Prostrate yourself (at least in your mind) as you say your morning prayers.
❏ Remember, "Without you, Lord, we can do nothing" (See John 15:5).
❏ Gaze up at the stars before evening prayers. Stand in awe.
❏ Bow your head and exclaim with the apostle Thomas, *My Lord and my God* (John 20:28).
❏ Sing a verse of "How Great Thou Art."
❏ Never make fun of or put down another person.

2) Reconciliation

❏ Say "I'm sorry" as often as is necessary.
❏ Say "I forgive you," even if the harming person doesn't apologize.
❏ Regarding hurts from the past, let bygones be bygones—especially forgive your parents.
❏ Say a prayer for those who have hurt you.
❏ If there is someone with whom you are not speaking, make efforts to be reconciled.
❏ Receive the Sacrament of Reconciliation.

3) Hospitality

❑ Smile.

❑ Cut back on the use of the word "I." Instead say, "Tell me more."

❑ Listen with all your senses and give others your total attention when they speak.

❑ Get rid of all prejudice.

❑ Envision your heart opening up and saying "Welcome" when you meet someone new.

❑ Have a supply of food and drink available in your home for unexpected visitors.

❑ Make sure the public areas of your home are clean and neat, not only for visitors, but also for the comfort of family members.

❑ Volunteer to help clean or decorate your church.

❑ Look at name-tags and call the waiter, the bus driver, the clerk, the toll booth person, etc. by name. If they have no name-tag, ask their name. Then say it out loud along with a word of thanks or a positive comment about their name, their smile, or their service.

4) Listening

❑ On Monday, read the Scripture selections for the coming Sunday.

❑ Discuss the Scripture with family and friends.

❑ Join a Bible study group.

❑ Teach catechism or help lead an RCIA group.

❑ Find a place to meditate and listen to your heart.

❑ Tell someone what the Lord has taught you from your mistakes.

❑ Take a trip to a natural history museum, a planetarium, or a botanical garden—study creation.

❑ Take a trip to an art museum and contemplate beauty.

❑ Take a trip to a national park and look, touch, smell, and listen. When you leave, say, "Thanks be to God," or "Praise to you, Lord Jesus Christ."

❑ Listen to the observations of children.

5) Petitions

❏ From the news you hear or read, list the problems that need special prayers this week. List the needs of the world, the nation, and the local community.

❏ Name three leaders in the world, nation, church (e.g. your pastor!) who need prayers.

❏ List the current difficulties that family and friends face and bring those needs to the altar on Sunday?

❏ List the sick you wish to include in your prayers?

❏ List any recently deceased members of your family or parish?

❏ Tell someone about your hopes and dreams.

6) Gratitude

❏ Read selections of the Passion narrative in the gospels.

❏ Reflect on *God so loved the world...* (John 3:16).

❏ Sing the "Holy, Holy, Holy" acclamation from Mass when you drive.

❏ There's a book, *14,000 Things to be Happy About* by Barbara Kipfer—make your own list. Come up with at least a thousand, and take your time.

❏ Write a "thank you" note to your parents, your teachers, and other significant people who were foundational in your life.

❏ Say a prayer of thanks for all your deceased relatives, friends, and parishioners. Visit their graves, and remember.

7) Transformation

❏ Be open to change, to conversion, to growth, to a passage, to a from-death-to-life experience.

❏ Reflect upon areas of your life that have been transformed, where good character traits and habits have set in. Then give thanks.

❑ Think about what areas of your life still need growth and development.

❑ Reflect upon areas of our world where good things are happening. Give thanks.

❑ Think about areas of the world that still needs to be transformed. For example, think of places that need food, clean water, sanitation, protection of the environment, etc. Pray for the end of all wars and terrorism.

❑ Pray for all missionaries who risk their lives to preach and bring Christ to the world.

8) Commitment

❑ Begin each day with the words, *Father, into your hands I commend my spirit* (Luke 23:46).

❑ Imagine Jesus asking you, "Do you love me?" Respond with a resounding "Yes, Lord, you know that I do."

❑ Renew your vows to your spouse or to your religious community.

❑ Recite the Apostles Creed.

❑ Recite the Pledge of Allegiance.

❑ Keep your promises.

9) Service

❑ Make a list of special talents God has given you.

❑ Reflect on how you can best use those talents, gifts, and abilities.

❑ If you aren't already a volunteer for a worthy cause, think of the possibilities. Also you can go to: www.catholicvolunteering.org & www.volunteermatch.org.

❑ Seek out those who are lonely or depressed. Listen to their story. Don't judge or advise. Just listen and understand.

❑ Become known as the one who speaks hope and a word of encouragement.

❏ Acknowledge and praise the good you see in others—anything noteworthy from good work, faithfulness, appearance, accomplishments, etc.
❏ Look for new ways to make life fun for others.

10) Compassion
❏ Imagine yourself as one of the homeless, the hungry, the victims of natural disasters, or those in war-torn countries.
❏ Imagine life or a mile in their shoes. Fill in the blank in your journal: *What would it be like....*
❏ Make watching the news, or reading the newspaper a time of prayer for those in pain.
❏ Feel compassion.
❏ Express your compassion.
❏ Act on your compassion.

The Eucharist must become the Center of our lives. Anyone who has really discovered Christ must lead others to Him. This is a joy we must not keep to ourselves. It must be passed on. —Benedict XVI

Personal Reflection:

Noted Resources

Benedict XVI
Sacramentum Caritatis: Pope Benedict XVI, apostolic exhortation on the Eucharist, March 13, 2007.

John Paul II
Mane Nobiscum Domine, Apostolic Letter for the Year of the Eucharist, October 7, 2004.

Homily, Mass and Eucharistic Procession, for the Solemnity of the Body and Blood of Christ, June 10, 2004 (Announces the "Year of the Eucharist").

Ecclesia de Eucharistia, Encyclical Letter on the Eucharist, April 17, 2003.

Dies Domini, On Keeping the Lord's Day, May 31, 1998.

Pope Paul VI
Mysterium Fidei, Encyclical on the Holy Eucharist, September 3, 1965.

Synod of Bishops, XI Ordinary General Assembly
The Eucharist: Source and Summit of the Life and Mission of the Church, Lineamenta, February 25, 2004.

Vatican Documents
General Instruction of the Roman Missal, Congregation for Divine Worship. Third typical edition, 2002.

Inaestimabile Donum, Instruction Concerning Worship of the Eucharistic Mystery, Sacred Congregation for the Sacraments and Divine Worship, April 17, 1980.

Directory for Masses with Children, Congregation for Divine Worship, November 1, 1973.

Eucharisticum Mysterium, Instruction on Eucharistic Worship, Sacred Congregation of Rites (May 25, 1967).

Sacrosanctum Concilium, Constitution on the Sacred Liturgy, Second Vatican Council, Promulgated by Pope Paul VI (December 4, 1963)

USCCB Documents

Sing to the Lord: Music in Divine Worship, United States Conference of Catholic Bishops, Washington, D.C., 2008

Introduction to the Order of Mass, United States Conference of Catholic Bishops, Washington, D.C., 2003

Built on Living Stones: Art, Architecture and Worship, Bishops' Committee on the Liturgy, National Conference of Catholic Bishops, 2000.

Fulfilled in Your Hearing: The Homily in the Sunday Assembly, Bishops Committee on Priestly Life and Ministry, National Conference of Catholic Bishops, 1982.

Books

Sunday Mass Five Years from Now, Gabe Huck, Chicago: Liturgy Training Publications, 2001.

Gather Faithfully Together, A Guide for Sunday Mass. Pastoral Letter of Cardinal Roger Mahony, Los Angeles, Sept 4, 1997.

The Liturgy Documents, A Parish Resource, Chicago: Liturgy Training Publications, 1991.

Strong, Loving and Wise: Presiding in Liturgy, Robert W. Hovda, Collegeville, MN: The Liturgical Press, 1976-1980.

The Mass of the Roman Rite: Its Origins and Development, Joseph A. Jungmann, S.J., New York, Benziger, Bros., 1959.

About the Author

Father Alan Phillip, C.P, is a Catholic priest and member of the Passionist Religious Congregation. He received his Masters of Divinity from St. Meinrad School of Theology in St. Meinrad, Indiana, and has pursued further theological studies at the Catholic Theological Union in Chicago, Illinois.

Since his ordination in 1967, Fr. Alan has served as Associate Pastor at Immaculate Conception parish in Chicago, Illinois, and as Pastor at St. Agnes Parish in Louisville, Kentucky. He has also worked at the Passionist Retreat Centers in Detroit, Michigan, and Warrenton, Missouri. Presently he resides at the Passionist Retreat Center in Sierra Madre, California, conducts Parish missions and retreats, and assists at the retreat center and at local parishes.

Father Alan accents the positive in his life and in the lives of others. Below Father Alan shares the personal insights and convictions that motivate his positive practices:

> "A person's self-image affects his or her ability to hope, dream, dare, and achieve. I seek to encourage and build the self-worth of another through common sense, the teachings of faith, and unconditional acceptance. And I do that in practical ways through my preaching, writing, and photography. I continually assure people of the beauty and goodness of God's creation—especially the human person."

Other Books & Materials by the author:

BOOKS

FROM BLUES TO JOY TO SMILES: Practical Steps to a Happier Life!

MY LEGACY: A Do-It-Yourself Book—
Document Your Journey & Share You Lessons

CD

The Inspirational Photography of Alan Phillip

To Contact Father Alan:

Fr. Alan Phillip, C.P.
Passionist Community
700 N. Sunnyside Ave.
Sierra Madre, CA 91024

Visit Father Alan online: http://www.alanphillipcp.com.
Here's what you'll find:
- information about Father Alan and his work;

- calendar of Fr. Alan's travel, book-signing, speaking, workshops, conferences, and ministry events;

- free newsletter articles (past-n-present) on many vital issues—all with Fr. Alan's wisdom, compassion, and hope;

- online bookstore to purchase all of Fr. Alan's published materials (books, ebooks, audiobooks, and photoCD).